COURANT
COMPUTER SCIENCE
SYMPOSIUM 1
JUNE 29 - JULY 1, 1970

DEBUGGING TECHNIQUES IN LARGE SYSTEMS

Edited by RANDALL RUSTIN

Courant Institute of Mathematical Sciences
New York University

PRENTICE-HALL, INC., Englewood Cliffs, New Jersey

ISBN: 0-13-197319-3

Library of Congress Catalog Card No.: 78-169618

10 9 8 7 6 5 4 3 2 1

Printed in United States of America

PRENTICE-HALL INTERNATIONAL, INC., London
PRENTICE-HALL OF AUSTRALIA, PTY. LTD., Sydney
PRENTICE-HALL OF CANADA, LTD., Toronto
PRENTICE-HALL OF INDIA PRIVATE LIMITED, New Delhi
PRENTICE-HALL OF JAPAN, INC., Tokyo

CONTENTS

Foreword

Introduction

List of Participants

Jacob T. Schwartz
An Overview of Bugs   1

Jim King
A Verifying Compiler   17

Harlen Mills
Top Down Programming in Large Systems   41

Ralph Grishman
Criteria for a Debugging Language   57

H. E. Kulsrud
*Extending the Interactive Debugging
   System HELPER*   77

Jim Blair
Extendable Non-Interactive Debugging   93

Robert M. Supnik
Debugging Under Simulation   117

W. R. Elmendorf
Disciplined Software Testing   137

Paul Schlender
*Application of Disciplined Software
   Testing*   141

N. J. King
Testing Conversational Systems   ,143

R. Stockton Gaines
Compiler Construction for Debugging   147

FOREWORD

The series of books of which the present volume
is the first originated in a symposium series in
areas of current interest in computer science which
the Computer Science Department of the Courant
Institute of Mathematical Sciences of New York University has presented since the summer of 1970.
Each symposium was devoted to a particular subject
area. Participants and speakers were drawn from
the academic and industrial communities, in accordance with an intent that the symposia should serve
for the interchange of ideas between these two
groups. The group of participants was normally
kept quite small, and selected for knowledge of and
active involvement in the fields to be discussed,
thus facilitating an informal flow of information.

Support for the meetings was provided by a
grant from the Mathematics Program of the Office of
Naval Research. I would like to thank Dr. Leila
Bram for her interest in and involvement with the
symposium series whose results are to be reported
in the series of volumes which follow; and Professor
Jacob T. Schwartz who was responsible for the general conception of the series and the choice of
specific topics.

I would also like to express my gratitude to
Miss Connie Engle, without whose administrative and
assistance this volume would not exist; and to
Miss Connie Engle without whose administrative and
organizational help I fear the symposium would not
have existed.

Randall Rustin

INTRODUCTION

This volume deals with efforts at control
and extermination of that notorious form of non-
insect life which we in the programming community
refer to, somewhat contemptuously, as "bugs."
Although as individuals we may in less cautious
moments speak of bugs with cavalier disdain, it is
always with a latent awareness that such bravado
may be the harbinger of a period of intense bug-
hunting, relieved only by occasional naps on piles
of discarded dumps. To the bug-plagued victim, the
sympathetic nods of one's colleagues more often
suggest relief that it is "him rather than me."

The more fatalistic among us may find such a
period good for the soul; a penance for the general
malfeasance of those involved in activity in which
a quantity of intellectual self-indulgence is toler-
ated. Of course, even given the frustration of the
exterminating effort, there is the pleasure in
locating and ridding a program of the infecting
source. The gratification of discovery could only
be enhanced at finding the bug was someone else's.

The content of the first paper, Jacob Schwartz's
"An Overview of Bugs," is readily deduced from its
title. It is a rather broad survey of the nature
and habitat of bugs. It may be read as an "overview"
of the present volume, and as a pointer toward
further developments and suggestions for research
in the field.

The other talks may be grouped (rather arbitrarily) according to the intentions of the authors
which are:

1. To develop procedures capable of guaranteeing
that programs are free of bugs; Jim King's paper is
representative of this group.

2. To make it possible to construct programs in a

style tending to avoid or at least to isolate bugs.
Work of this kind will be of particular interest to
those groups involved in the production of large
programming systems. Harlan Mills' paper sets forth
a view of hierarchical program structure intended to
be useful in such environments.

3. To apply a strongly disciplined testing technique to large systems during their development.
W.R. Elmendorf and Paul Schlender discuss various
issues related to testing. Nick King discusses the
manner in which the testing of a large-scale time-
sharing system (TSS) was handled.

4. To describe methods for the detection of bugs
in particular environments. This group of papers
by Jim Blair, Ralph Grishman, H. E. Kulsrud, Robert
Supnik and R. Stockton Gaines give detailed specifications of various debugging systems, relating these
to the operating systems under which they run and the
languages in connection with which they will be
used.

Finally, the word "large" in "The Debugging
and Maintenance of Large Software Systems" stresses
the organizers' special interest in debugging of
highly complex programming systems. A less formi-
dable, and considerably more succinct title, might
have been "Expunging the Ubiquitous Bug." But
perhaps this would have smacked too much of wish
fulfillment.

                    Randall Rustin

PARTICIPANTS

Allen, Frances	New York University
Andrieu, Joyce	Allen-Babcock Computing, Inc.
Baskin, Herbert B.	University of California
Blair, Jim	Purdue University
Brady, John	University of Toronto
Burghard, Kent	IBM Mohansic Systems Lab.
Burns, Sharon L.	Kaiser Foundation, California
Casey, Keven B.	Catholic University of America
Ching, Stephen W.	Villanova University
Christensen, Ken	IBM, Poughkeepsie
Christy, Peter	Computer Science Corporation
Dalphin, John F.	Purdue University
Desautels, E.J.	University of Wisconsin
Elmendorf, W.R.	IBM
Feldman, Marshall	Mass. Institute of Technology
Firedman, Jerry M.	Brookhaven National Laboratory
Fuchel, Kurt	Brookhaven National Laboratory
Gaines, R. Stockton	Institute for Defense Analysis
Glickman, Daniel	EDP Wares, Inc., NYC
Goldstein, M.	New York University
Grishman, R.	Courant Institute
Haggerty, Joseph P.	Bell Telephone Labs., Whippany
Hansen, Wilfred	Argonne National Laboratory
Harris, Arthur D.S.	Brookhaven National Laboratory
Heller, Sidney	Brookhaven National Laboratory
Highland, Harold J.	S.U.N.Y., Farmingdale
Hochberg, Mark	Columbia University
Horwitz, Richard	Brookhaven National Laboratory
Johnson, Beverly R.	Columbia University
Keim, Joseph W.	University of Dayton, Ohio
King, Jim	IBM
King, N.J.	IBM, Systems Development Div.
Klouda, Kenneth W.	University of Akron, Ohio
Kulsrud, Helene	Institute for Defense Analysis
Kuo, Shan S.	University of New Hampshire
Lawrence, Leslie L.	Brookhaven National Laboratory
Lippert, John R.	Pennsylvania State University
London, Ralph L.	University of Wisconsin
Loveman, David B.	Wright-Patterson AFB, Ohio
McManus, John J.	M.I.T.
Mills, H.D.	IBM, Federal Systems Division
Halaris, Antony S.	Iona College, N.Y.

Nicholls, Robert E.	M.I.T., Lincoln Laboratory
Ostrinsky, Renah	Brooklyn College
Pagan, Frank	University of Toronto
Paige, Robert A.	New York University
Pasachoff, Nancy W.	Barnard College
Ragusa, Florence	New York University
Ramm, Dietolf	Duke University Medical Ctr.
Rice, Edward H.	John Hopkins University
Ringquist, Barbara	OCAMA, Tinker AFB, Oklahoma
Schlender, Paul	IBM
Schwartz, J.T.	Courant Institute
Shneiderman, B.	S.U.N.Y., Stoneybrook
Smith, Alison	New York University
Sondak, Norman E.	Worchester Polytechnic Inst.
Supnik, Robert M.	Applied Data Research
Yeh, James	UNIVAC, Washington, D.C.

AN OVERVIEW OF BUGS

Jacob T. Schwartz
Courant Institute of Mathematical Sciences
New York University

A survey of the type, frequency, and habitat of bugs is outlined. Debugging tools presently available are discussed and suggestions for their development advanced. The role of "proofs of program correctness" and the debugging process itself are discussed.

I am informed at second-hand that, early in the history of computers, and more precisely at that moment of high drama when the Whirlwind I at M.I.T. was first switched on, it failed to run. A frantic check of the wiring, complex for its time, began at once — but yielded nothing. Finally, a thought broke through the panic: perhaps it was the program, that simple thing of paper only, rather than the formidable-looking hardware that was at fault. So it was; and from the ancestor thus discovered we may consider the hosts of bugs that plague all our programming efforts to be descended.

There can be things wrong with programs — in fact, very seriously wrong. The presence in programs of bugs can be regarded as a fundamental phenomenon; the bug-free program as an abstract theoretical

concept like the absolute zero of thermodynamics,
which can be envisaged but never attained. Thus,
bugs and debugging are to be studied very seriously.
In order to structure the very disorganized but
important subject of the present symposium, I wish
to note the principal sub-headings under which the
parts of this area might be grouped.

A first area might be called entomology: the
study of bugs by observation. This study might begin
with the classification of bugs by type. Anyone who
has done much debugging will have built up a personal
collection of typical bugs. Such a list is helpful
in one's own debugging, indicating what to look for
on first encountering trouble. This list will vary
with programmer experience and also with the stage
of debugging. Array over-write is a prime specimen
in any collection. Another subspecies of importance
is the "off by 1" group which may be divided into
two principal subfamilies: off by 1 in indexing,
and off by 1 in shifting, which is related to the
more general class of "wrong flag bit" bug. Next
we may note the initialization bugs, manifest in
situations in which things fail to have either the
initial or the terminal value which a programmer
expects. Yet another group are the "operation
irregularity" bugs, introduced by the inevitable
fact that computer arithmetic is never of infinite
precision, so that, for example, at the ends of their
range, twos-complement arithmetic and ones-comple-
ment arithmetic don't work in the way an unsuspect-
ing programmer imagines. These are a few principal
troublemakers. What is their distribution in
ordinary debugging experience? It would be quite
interesting to know.

All the bugs just noted are creatures of the
early phases of debugging. Beyond these there
exists a whole class of bugs, belonging to the later
stage of debugging, which may be called *situational*
bugs. A bug of this kind, normally infesting
operating systems, may be called the *semaphore bug*,
manifest wherever a process A is waiting upon a
process B while process B is waiting upon process A.
Bugs of this kind can only emerge later in the

debugging of complex systems; they only appear once
most systems processes begin to work. Still more
elusive are the whole class of *timing bugs*, which
are often subtle evanescent versions of their
semaphore cousins.

As has been said, it would be most interesting
to develop a systematic completion of this sketchy
list and to supplement it with a careful statistical
study of bugs typical for the various stages of
debugging, so as to try to provide a clearer picture
of the debugging experience. In the present state of
of our subject, I doubt that anyone at this symposium will succeed very well in doing this. However,
we will have talks by people used to dealing with
bugs *en masse* administratively and who have extensive
data bases on debugging situations. They may be able
to provide some facts. Generally, however, facts
concerning bugs are recorded only in late stages of
debugging and very often only after programs have
been field-released. Information concerning the
much more numerous early bugs is most often completely lost in the hurly-burly of initial debugging.

Next, we may enquire into various aspects of
the habitat of bugs. For example, it is interesting
to ask what types of *language features* are most bug-
prone. We may, e.g., note one type of bug, often
catastrophic in its effects, which is typically
associated with the use of pointers; on encountering
such a bug, one often transfers off to nowhere or
begins writing into some strange place in a program.
Similarly, the remark has often been made that the
number of bugs in a program is proportional to the
number of labels which it contains. This remark
cannot possibly be true as it stands since there are
mechanical algorithms for converting any arbitrary
program into one in which there are no labels; the
application of this algorithm surely cannot be a
magical debugging method. Nevertheless, the remark
is common enough and reasonable enough to be worth
pondering. In all these matters statistics and hard
information would be most interesting.

Were it possible to collect this information,

the process of bug extermination, which is to say the
application of debugging tools, could be viewed in
a more confident way. Lacking this information, we
proceed anyhow to discuss debugging tools. With
regard to these tools, a useful subclassification
according to the stage of debugging at which they
are aimed can be made. Quite different situations
are faced in early and in late debugging. The sort
of tools useful for early debugging are by now rather
familiar. They include, in the first place, traces
at various levels; whether the transfer level, or the
subroutine level, or various selective levels, together with various kinds of traps, various kinds of
dumps, and various kinds of program-termination
summaries, such as an account of the number of statements executed or of the particular statements
executed in a program run. All these debugging tools
relate in an interesting way to the fundamental
question of language level. Assuming that one is
writing in a high-level language, do the debugging
tools at one's disposal enable one to get summary and
dump information at that language level, or is this
information provided at some lower level of language,
i.e., in some machine language form which has to be
converted painfully to mean something in a higher-
level language like FORTRAN?

     This question is an instance of the interesting
and more general problem of tool usability. Normally, at the beginning of the debugging process,
even a programmer with some past experience can never
believe how bad things are really going to be before
the end. Perhaps this is a merciful veil cast over
the situation by beneficent higher powers. Nevertheless, the prevalence of this illusion means that one
never introduces quite as many debugging aids as at
the end of an experience one wishes one had. In
particular, one rarely is willing to pick up and use
heavy debugging tools, and, for example, one finds
it very annoying in debugging to have to write masses
of format statements to get fragmentary dumps. I
think therefore that in designing early-stage debugging tools the question of tool usability is very
important. One wants tools which will produce debugging information without requiring that many

extra statements be written. One is also fearful
about introducing things into a program which may
cause bugs when they are removed. All of these
considerations highlight the important question of
tool usability, a question which I hope the
speakers who are going to talk about early-stage
debugging tools will address.

Early-stage debugging tools are normally used
in connection with relatively small programs, which
may perhaps be pieces of large programs, but which
are pieces being developed separately prior to an
integration phase in which these pieces, which may
all seem to be working well, are combined. Upon
this combination many late-stage bugs generally make
their appearance; one then requires tools for dealing with bugs in large complex systems. During
this symposium we may hope to hear a good deal about
some of the tools which have been developed for debugging in this situation. Perhaps, however, it is
well to take a pessimistic view of these bugs.
Nobody really knows what to do about them. Nevertheless there have been some interesting technique
fragments developed under the pressure of desperate
necessity. These include a certain number of ideas
in the area of systematic program testing. After
one has run a set of tests against a compiler or
against a large operating system, one wants to know
how thoroughly the range of situations that might
arise has been explored. A rather pessimistic
general answer is possible; the range of possible
situations, being enormous, has not been explored
thoroughly at all. Nevertheless, one wants to make
sure that at least some kind of *systematic* super-
ficial coverage has been attained; to ensure this,
one uses such measurement yardsticks as the percent
of code that has actually been executed during test,
the percent of the total number of branches that has
been taken in both directions during test, etc.
Several later talks will cover this point. It
would be well to try to extend these notions of
statistical coverage to something more situational,
which might, for instance, give some account of the
extent to which various interlock situations had
been explored, etc. Perhaps something could be

done in this direction by careful program structuring
associated with some systematic view of the segmentation of a composite system into subparts and of
the degree to which these subparts interact. Such
a segmentation tool would be interesting; we have
none.

After late-stage debugging is past, the various
evanescent bugs make their fitful appearance, flitt-
ing in and out. Here part of the problem is simply
to capture them as they fly by, and get some idea of
what has happened in one or another mysterious
situation which may seem to have appeared and then
gone away. We may hear some account of what is being
done to deal with such particularly vexing problems,
particularly in regard to the field reporting of
mysterious events and the ways that one attempts to
capture information concerning such events.

Next we may raise the general question of
program structure for bug-proofing. Under this
heading a number of remarks may be made. First of
all, there is a question of language level. If one
had a reliable classification of bugs, allowing
certain of them to be associated with certain levels
of language, then one could say with some degree of
confidence that by passing to a higher level of
language various kinds of bugs would be eliminated.
It is, for example, clear that if you write in
FORTRAN you don't have to worry about register bugs,
unless of course one writes in a FORTRAN allowing
one to deal explicitly with registers. On the other
hand, in coding at the FORTRAN level, one does, for
example, have to worry about the "off by 1" type
of bug and the various kinds of initialization bugs.
These in turn might be eliminated in a language of
a still higher level, in which, instead of using
explicit iterations, one used a logical set concept
and just said, "Do this process for all the elements
of the set S." In this sense, the progress (or is
it a retreat?) of languages to higher levels may aid
debugging substantially.

Beyond these questions on the level of language
there has been a certain amount of speculation

recently concerning the informal but systematic
structuring of programs to avoid bugs. A recent
paper by Dijkstra has excited interest; in it he
reports on an operating system which he calls THE,
in which a number of bugs were apparently avoided
by systematic use of a type of design which might
be called a "layered macrostructure design." In
building this operating system, and starting with
the true machine facilities, Dijkstra's group first
constructed from these facilities a number of
logical macros, essentially an operating system
language at a slightly higher level. These macros
were checked out very carefully and also were kept
transparent by being held to a very small size.
This created a macro language the next level of
the system is built using these macros exclusively.
This created a macro language; the next level of
the system is built using these macros exclusively.
The next system level consists in turn of a set of
structure, a total system is obtained, with, it is
claimed, a high degree of freedom from bugs. Now,
whereas any claim of good results is to be taken
suspiciously, and whereas it is particularly to be
noted concerning the experiment described that one
is dealing with a relatively small system, it must
nevertheless be admitted that Dijkstra's basic idea
is a good one.

    Another thought belonging to the same general
area is that of confining the effects of bugs, an
of an idea." But "error-tolerant software," when
said to oneself, is indeed a marvelous phrase, and
some years ago about a mathematical subject (dynamic
programming), "There goes a wonderful name in search
of an idea." But error-tolerant software, when said
to oneself, is indeed a marvelous phrase, and
perhaps one that actually has some content. If, for
example, one considers an operating system in which
various data structures are involved, one may note
first of all that damage to one of these data
structures may be of minor consequence, while damage
to another may be very serious. Thus, if in a time-
sharing system one loses a master file table, the
consequences may be catastrophic. If one simply
loses the scheduling table, that is, simply loses

information concerning programs currently being
executed, the consequences may be minor, since it
may be possible to "refresh" the system by erasing
this whole table and rescheduling every job. Next,
note that one may be able to recover from the
potentially catastrophic event of file table loss
if information concerning file ownership has been
kept with the files themselves. One has then only
to go out onto the discs and look in the files in
order to reconstruct the file catalog. This is the
sort of thing a librarian could do and would do if
some nameless few came in and threw all a library's
file catalogs out the window. If such ideas are
kept in mind, it may be possible to create system
designs embodying a certain measure of redundancy.
One would have to keep a careful eye on such questions as the following: What modules are writing
in what areas? What will be the consequences of an
error in one or another program or data field?
What reconstruction procedures will remain workable?

       Beyond all these ideas lies the theoretical
El Dorado of debugging, to which at least a few of
our speakers will address themselves, namely the
idea of proving program correctness by formal mathematical methods. The application of some such
method would eventually yield an assertion that
program X is certified error-free on a basis of
mathematical proof. This is an interesting idea
which a number of people (including John McCarthy and
his collaborators; Bob Floyd; and various others
inspired by their initial efforts) have begun to
explore. This idea, worked out, would have major
consequences for debugging. For the time being one
would, in fact, be very happy with any partial
success. In order to justify this pessimistic
opinion, I shall mention a few reasons which lead
me to believe that proving program correctness is
going to be a very difficult thing to do much about.
In the first place, the formally stated problem,
"to prove programs correct," has as a special case
the general problem of proving algorithms equivalent.
Now, this latter problem is, in the technical, mathematical sense, unsolvable. This is bad enough,
but, still worse, the algorithm equivalence problem

is unsolvable in a very strong sense. More precisely, there does not exist any finite set of axioms
from which proofs can be elaborated to cover all
possible cases of algorithm equivalence. Thus, like
mathematics itself, the study of algorithm equivalence must remain an ever-developing subject in
which new proof methods are from time to time
developed.

The methods which until now have been suggested
for proving program correctness can be classified
under two headings: on the one hand, axiomatic
proofs of algorithm equivalence; on the other hand,
one has an approach suggested by Bob Floyd — a quite
interesting approach — with approximately the
following structure. After writing down a program
P, one writes down a set of statements concerning
the situation expected to prevail at each point of
the program. That is, one writes a set of formal
annotations, attaching such annotations to each
statement or each principal node in the program P.
These annotations assert that at such-and-such a
point, such-and-such a situation must hold. When
the set of annotations is complete, one invokes a
formal device, having the nature of a specialized
theorem-proving algorithm, which, looking at all
these annotations, establishes the fact that
collectively they imply each other, and hence that
they are logically implied by some initial assertion
guaranteed to hold on entrance to the program. This
method then furnishes a formal, logical proof of
the correctness of the annotations written, provided
that the program P is entered with data of the type
specified. Adding some way of guaranteeing program
termination, one can hope to assert that P is proven
correct.

It is worth emphasizing that, in order for such
an assertion to be relatively decisive, the proofs
to which we refer must be checked by a formal
algorithmic mechanism. It is not enough to give
formal mathematical proof, i.e., a proof certified
by a mathematician, because mathematical proofs, as
mathematicians well know, also contain bugs. By
giving an informal mathematical proof one might

merely have transferred existing bugs to another
place. In the process, of course, one would
probably have reduced the number of surviving bugs:
in fact, Floyd has reported from personal experience
that in systematically trying to prove the correctness of programs he finds many bugs; informal
attempts to prove the correctness of a program
amount to a kind of disciplined desk-checking.
Nevertheless, if one rests one's case upon an
informal proof, even one that several people have
read, one does not have anything that really amounts
to a guarantee of correctness. I think here of a
case that became famous in mathematics a few years
ago, in which after certain statements in algebraic
number theory had been proven by three independent
methods in published papers (an algebraic proof,
an analytic proof, and an elementary proof), a
counter-example was published.

        I don't mean to make this point too strongly,
since serious efforts at formal proof of program
correctness would surely succeed in lowering the
number of bugs remaining in programs. Moreover,
a very interesting type of debugging aid is
suggested by Floyd's correctness-proof methods.
This idea is as follows: one can implement a system
by which a programmer, during the process of
program elaboration, could formally state those
assumptions concerning the moment-to-moment state
of his data which led him to write his program as
he did. Such a system might be in the form of a
language in which assumptions could be declared, say,
by including *assumption* statements among the other
statements of a program. Then, simply by entering
a "debug mode," these assumptions could be checked
dynamically; reports on erroneous assumptions
could be generated automatically. For example, in
a sufficiently powerful assumption language, one
might state that at the end of a program loop
intended to clear an array it was assumed that all
elements of the array were zero. If this assumption
failed, a most useful report stating that some
element of the array was still not zero could be
generated.

To return, however, to the stricter formal proof idea, which I now take in its "strong form," i.e., as the idea of producing sets of formal annotations whose logical completeness and correctness can actually be verified by an algorithm. Even accepting the optimistic view that this could be done, it is still to be feared that the necessary proofs might often grow very complicated. Such proofs can be complicated even if we work with idealized programs dealing with the integers of mathematics rather than the integers of computing, i.e., work with objects that are an unlimited number of bits long rather than things that will overflow at the thirty-second bit. And, of course, logical gaps like the ones just mentioned often become fertile breeding grounds for bugs. If formal proof mechanisms have to take such detailed difficulties into account, as they must if they are to guarantee the assertion that a particular program P was going to run correctly, not only on a hypothetical machine with infinitely long integers, but actually on the machine for which P was developed, then one might have to write very complex proofs indeed. Worst of all, it might be found that in order to produce proofs a programmer had to write enormous masses of annotations. The proposed proof method might therefore, in the absence of developments which are not now in sight, break down under its own weight. Most pessimistically of all, one can assert that the present debugging process is precisely an informal proof procedure, during which a programmer tries to convince himself, on the basis of certain reasonings and certain empirical tests, that his program is correct, spot-checking his arguments as he goes along.

Some theoretical reflections upon the debugging process itself may also help us to understand why certain tools are more likely to be useful than others. Debugging always starts with some evidence of program failure. This may be the appearance in an output file of some recognizably unreasonable result, or may be some system-monitored error event: time-out, illegal storage reference, illegal operation. An erroneous result of this sort is, of

course, evidence of the existence of a program error
somewhere in the program being run, and the problem
in debugging is to work one's way back from the
visible symptom to this program error. Program
errors are wrongly stated operations or groups of
operations, and their immediate consequence is the
transformation of a collection of reasonable inputs
into an output unreasonable in some regard. Thus,
hypothetically considering the whole history of a
computation up to the point at which obvious evidence of error develops, we seek in debugging to
search out those key steps in which a reasonable
set of arguments has been used to produce an unreasonable result. The problem of course is that
the definitions of "reasonable" and "unreasonable"
to be applied go back to those vaguely formulated
assumptions made by the programmer responsible for
a program under debugging, assumptions which in one
sense or another make him believe that the program
ought to work properly. To the extent that these
assumptions are vaguely formulated, they must be
applied during the debugging process, not mechanically, but by a human programmer capable of re-
defining his assumptions inductively while surveying
miscellaneous evidence. On the other hand, the
history of an extensive computation constitutes a
vast mass of data, which a human programmer is
incapable of surveying comprehensively. The debugging process therefore aims to be the exploration of as narrow a vein as possible within the
total history of a computation, with the intent of
locating an operation transforming reasonable arguments into an unreasonable result.

Having stated this general view of the debugging
process, it is well to consider two principal
"dimensions" of the total program history which
must be explored during debugging: the dimension of
space and the dimension of time. The space dimension of a program history is measured by the extent
and complexity of the data structures which interact
within it. The time dimension of a program history
is measured by the number of cycles of computation
which it represents. Now, most computations are
significantly longer in the time than in the space

dimension; this is true in the sense that computations normally run long enough to modify the whole of the memory available to them several hundreds of times over. Moreover, most programming languages, and even those which allow the definition of fairly complex data structures, do not allow complex structures to interact directly with each other on a composite basis, but only allow interactions on an "entry-by-entry" basis. Thus, in debugging, one can normally reason back, following a chain of defective entries on a time-path that is long but not spatially extended, and without ordinarily having to consider the global structure of very complex entities. (Exceptions to this observation might be SNOBOL and LISP, especially the latter.) Moreover, since the memory space available to computations is normally much smaller than the time available to them, programs will almost inevitably be biased toward the use of techniques in which results are developed by the progressive and iterative modification of data structures, limited in size but changing very dynamically. (A hypothetical exception here might be a large data-manipulation system, which made use of very extensive external memory, and in which computation was greatly slowed down by the burden of frequent access to external devices; note, however, that the few existing systems having this general description normally use data sets only of a primitive, highly regular structure.) The upshot of these observations is that debugging is normally much more an exploration along the time than along the space dimension of a defective computation. As soon as one is able to find, within the history of a computation, any definite anomaly which is not preceded by many cycles of computation also containing anomalies, one is normally quite close to the identification of an erroneous instruction. Debugging strategy therefore generally aims to work back, from whatever error has initially been noticed, to an earliest-occurring anomaly. We shall call this "first error" the *target anomaly* of the debugging process.

The difficulty normally faced when debugging

begins is that a large number of cycles will have
passed between the time of occurrence of the target
anomaly and the first occurrence of a visible error
symptom. If this has not led to destruction of
vital evidence concerning the target anomaly, it
may be possible to reason one's way back to the
target anomaly using nothing more than a complete
picture ("dump") of the program state at the time
the visible error symptom developed. If this is
not the case, more sophisticated techniques of back-
tracing must be employed. Note here what is true
more generally — that the debugging process will on
the average be simplified to the extent that initial
anomalies are likely to lead rapidly to system-
detectable symptoms. The more narrowly specified
is the path of reasonable possibilities open to a
program, the less likely it is that anomalous data
will be passively accepted. In this sense we may
expect that, e.g., APL programs, which work with
highly structured data, will from the start be
considerably easier to debug than programs written
at an irredundant machine level and prepared to
accept rather arbitrary bit patterns. Note also
that to increase the probability that anomalies will
lead rapidly to detectable symptoms, the formal,
redundant statement of programmer assumptions
considered above will be a valuable technique.

To move back from an error symptom to the
initially hidden anomalies which precede it, we may
start by examining a particular operation generating
an observed error symptom and look in detail at its
arguments. If, as usual, the error symptom initially
detected is not itself the target anomaly, then one
of the arguments of this operation will appear on
inspection to be anomalous and we will proceed to
inquire after the earlier operation which set this
argument, etc. Such stepwise back-tracking can,
in easy cases, lead in relatively short order to
the discovery of the target anomaly; however, all too
often it may simply lead to the discovery of a pro-
tracted iterative loop, in every step of which an
anomalous input leads to some anomalous output. To
surmount such a debugging obstacle, various techniques are available. It may be possible, by

surveying a pattern of repeated anomalies, to detect
some persistent anomalous condition. If this is the
case, one can try to find the first time this condition arose. Less specifically, one may be able to
surmise that a detected anomaly implies that certain
aspects of the behavior of a program probably have
an extended anomalous history. In this case, one
may produce a full or partial trace of certain hopefully relevant aspects of the program's history,
hoping that by visual inspection of such a trace an
early-occurring anomaly may be found, upon which
anomaly continued debugging may then more profitably
be based. As this empirical search-back process
goes on, one's confidence in certain sections may
fall under a cloud of suspicion. Sections considered suspicious can be separately re-examined or
exorcised. Eventually suspicion will focus success-
fully on an offending instruction.

       In the debugging process just outlined, one is
exploring the history of a computation along its
time dimension; what is desirable in order that
this process be effective is a powerful facility for
detecting certain key events within a total history.
For example, we may wish to find the last time prior
to a given occasion at which the value of a variable
was set, or the first time a given condition
occurred. What we therefore need is a language
whose fundamental entities are program events, and
which allows us to search for events or combinations
of events which we suspect to be anomalous and to
display information concerning these events. Such
an event-oriented debugging language seems to me to
be nascent in some of the debugging tools to be
described during this symposium. In accordance with
the appreciations developed above, this language
should look in both time directions; i.e., it should
allow one to search not only for the first occurrence of an event a after an event b, but also to
search for the last occurrence of an event a before
an event b. Such an ideal debugging language
should use the events which it detects to trigger
various programmed actions and to direct information
interactively to a programmer at a console.

Note that an event language of this kind will
also be useful for the analysis of bugs whose
symptoms are endless loops, rather than those which
lead to program collapse in finite time. A
programmer's hope that the loops in his program will
not be endless is normally based on some notion of
partial order implicit in his expectations concerning the course of a computation; each loop through
a program section is expected to advance the
program's data in a forward direction, i.e., to a
stage discernibly closer to the result which is
eventually to emerge. Thus, once the occurrence of
an endless loop has shown that a program is failing
in one sense or another to push its data consistently
forward, one may wish to search for the first
complete pass through a suspect loop which fails to
move forward in the expected sense, to try to find
those operations which supply the parameters
controlling this complex event, etc.

It should be recognized that a "program event
language" of the kind described, oriented to explor-
ations along the time axis of a program history,
may be *relatively* (but only relatively) less ade-
quate for use in connection with hypothetical
languages permitting very complex data items than
it would be in connection with a more conventional
programming language. Debugging programs written
in a language allowing large, highly structured
objects to interact with each other may involve
static exploration of data structures and of their
relationships to an unusual degree. This situation
being somewhat hypothetical, it is hard to antici-
pate precisely what techniques will turn out to be
useful in dealing with it. Dynamically, it is clear
that one might often wish to discover the last time
prior to a given event that some particular portions
of larger data objects were modified.

Beyond all our theoretical speculations there
lie some major practical questions. What do we do
about debugging in contexts in which hundreds of
people are at work on very large systems?   And,
what management aids are available for preventing
chaos in such situations?

A VERIFYING COMPILER

James King
Computer Science Department
IBM T. J. Watson Research Center

A program to be compiled is annotated with propositions about the relations among its variables. Consistency between these propositions and the actual program is proved automatically. Once "verified," the program is guaranteed to compute correct results. Unsuccessful verification provides clues as to the location and nature of any errors.

This talk is about debugging programs. However, it is a little different view of debugging than most of the previous talks. If the ideas presented here can be carried out in practice, debugging programs will be unnecessary because they will have already been proven correct. I am going to talk about a verifying compiler. This is a compiler that, in addition to compiling programs, allows you to prove that the program will always execute correctly.

Let us look at Figure 1, which is a picture of an interpretation of what compilers typically do today. We begin with the abstract concept of the computation to be performed. A programmer, after conceiving of the computation required, or

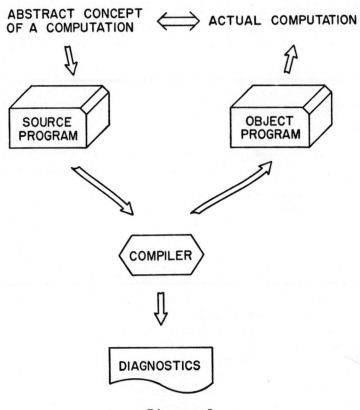

Figure 1

Typical Compiler

having been told what this concept is by verbal
description or a sketchy written report, translates
this report into a very precise formal notation in
a programming language. Now, the programming language is run through the compiler which, of course,
generates the object program which performs the
actual computation and, as a side effect, may produce diagnostics. These diagnostics have nothing
to do with the abstract concept of the computation,
but simply point out inconsistencies in the formal
notation of the programming language. This gives
you no check on the mapping between the abstract
concept and what actually gets computed. What we

would really like to do is get a better handle on
the problem of having the actual computation really
represent what the abstract concept was going to be.

     Now look at Figure 2. This is a picture of
what a verifying compiler would do. Now you'll
notice it does the same things that a regular,
typical compiler does, but, in addition to that, we

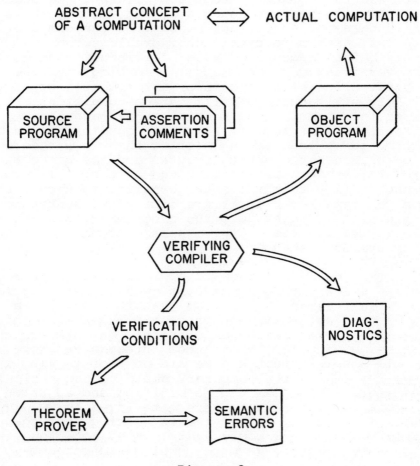

Figure 2

Verifying Compiler

have one more set of formal information that is
drawn from the programmer's concept of his computation. This is denoted as *assertion comments* in
the figure. These are symbolic predicates that
describe the behavior of the program in a different
way than the programming language does. The verifying compiler accepts both the source program and
these assertion comments, generates the object
program and the regular diagnostics, and, in addition,
it checks the consistency between the source program and the comments about the program. We now
have two independent sources of information about
the programmer's abstract concept of the computation
and can check more consistency problems than we
could before because we have additional information.
The verifying compiler is still working with the
consistencies among the information that's given to
it. It will generate verification conditions which
arise in comparing the source program and the
assertion comments. If all these conditions can be
proved to be true (by submitting them to a theorem
prover), then the source program and the comments
are at least consistent with one another. If you
cannot verify that these are consistent, then you
can generate semantic errors similar to syntactic
diagnostics. These help the programmer to change
the source program or the assertion comments so that
they are consistent.

        The best way I know to explain this material
in any brief period of time is by example. Figure 3
shows an interesting program, yet it's simple enough
to be used as an example in a brief talk like this.
This program is designed to operate on integers and
we assume, further, that these integers can take
on all possible values. We are now not talking in
a strict sense of a computer, but of a theoretical
computer. The ideas can be modified and adjusted
to work for actual computers with fixed precision,
but I'm primarily interested in getting over the
basic ideas, and I would just as soon not cloud the
issues by bringing in more complicated concepts.

        The way this program operates is to consider
the integer Y in its binary representation and

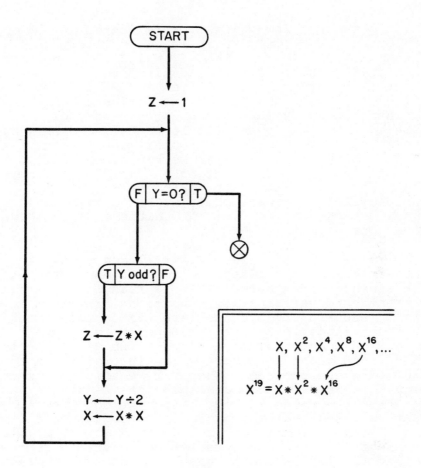

Figure 3

X To An Integer Power Y

generate successive powers of X as indicated in
Figure 3. For example, suppose we want to raise X
to the 19th power. The program generates X, X^2,
X^4, X^8, X^{16}, and so forth. We then choose those
powers in the sequence of powers of X that corre-
spond to one bits in the binary representation of Y.
In this case, for $Y=19_{10}=10011_2$, we want to multiply
together the 1st, 2nd, and 5th powers of X.

The right-most binary bit of Y is tested in the
statement, Is Y odd? If it is, we multiply the
appropriate power of X into Z, which is accumulating
the final result. Z is initialized to one. We
shift Y to put it in a position to examine the next
bit by dividing it by two. The divide symbol is to
be interpreted as taking the integer part of the
quotient and discarding the remainder. We know we
are finished with this particular computation whenever Y reaches zero because we have then shifted
off all the bits representing Y. This is a somewhat subtle algorithm for taking an integer to
another integer power. Yet, it has only a small
number of statements, and for that reason it serves
as a good example.

If we look at Figure 4, we'll see what the
program looks like after it has been annotated with
the assertion comments. (Please read the assertion
comments and verification conditions from left to
right, assuming the usual hierarchical relationships
of the arithmetic and logical operators.) The
assertion comment associated with the START denotes
those conditions for which we're interested in
executing the program. Whenever we initiate execution of this program, we assume that X has the value
A, Y has the value B, and $Y \geq 0$. We don't often
want to prove that a program is correct over all
possible inputs but only for those that are really
meaningful. The most interesting assertion is the
one at the end of the program because that charac-
terizes the final result we intended to compute.
In this case, we simply claim that $Z = A^B$ where A
and B are the values given in the initial assertion.
There we assumed initially that $X = A$ and $Y = B$.
This must be done because the values of X and Y are
modified by the program. We could not put the claim
that $Z = X^Y$ at the end of the program because that's
just not true. The values of Y and X have been
changed. By inventing the new symbols A and B on
the initial assertions, and by reusing them in the
final assertion, we have a notation for relating
the inputs and the outputs.

There is a third assertion on this program that
theoretically is not necessary, but practically is
very useful. This assertion is necessarily true
at its point of attachment in the program. By this
I mean, if you take the current execution values of
the variables that occur in the program at that
point and substitute into the assertion expression,
you will find that the expression evaluates to true.
This predicate, you'll notice, is on the loop of
the program and we refer to it as an *inductive
predicate*. It's an inductive predicate because it
allows us to make a proof of the correctness of
this program due to an inductive argument based on
the number of times you execute the loop. The
rules for including assertion comments in the program in order to make the method work are: (1) You
must have one at the end to define what you mean
by correctness of the program. (2) You may option-
ally put initial conditions on the program by
supplying the predicate at the beginning. (3) You
must cut every loop in the program by an inductive
predicate. It may turn out that one inductive
predicate will cut more than one loop in the program,
but at least every loop must be cut. We'll see the
motivation behind the inductive predicates as we
proceed.

You will notice that this program is now
composed of four paths of control, each of which
begins with a predicate (assertion comment) and ends
with a predicate. The first path consists of beginning with the initial predicate and going to the
inductive predicate, bracketing the statement
"z ← 1." That's the initialization portion of the
program.
Then you'll notice there are two paths around
the loop beginning at the inductive predicate,
executing a path around the loop and returning to
the inductive predicate. One way we multiply X
into Z, and the other way we don't. The fourth
and final path is from the inductive predicate out
to the final predicate.

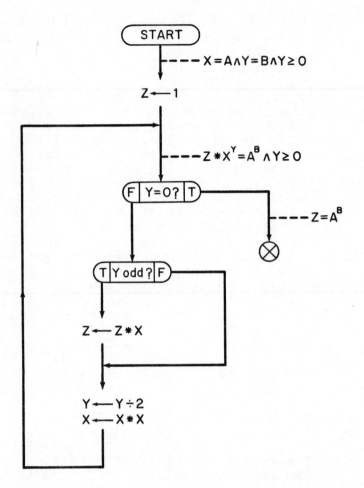

Figure 4

Suppose Initially X=A and Y=B

One of two essential ideas that I would like to get across today is this: By cutting every loop in the program with an inductive predicate, any execution

of this program can be composed of paths, in this
case, of four kinds. Any execution must begin with
the initial segment, followed by some combination
of the two paths around the loop, and eventually
have a terminating path going to the exit. The
purpose of the inductive predicate is thus to cut
the program into a fixed number of paths, in this
case four, which will cover any execution sequence
of the program. This is a key point because now we
wish to generate a proof for each one of these paths,
and claim that that constitutes a proof of correctness which will then apply for arbitrary executions
of the program.

Let me talk about the assertion comment as tag-
ging paths; we will call these four paths, tag paths.
A *tag path* is a path that has an assertion at the
beginning, follows the flow of the program, and has
an assertion at the end. We prove that the tag
paths are correct. That is, we show that whenever
the initial tag is true and we execute the interven-
ing statement, then the final tag will be true. We
have thus verified that path. This process results
in what we call *verification conditions*, one for
each tag path. If we can prove all of the verification conditions, and we've verified all of the tag
paths, then we have verified the program and proved
that it will always execute correctly.

If we look at Figure 5, we see there are four
verification conditions generated from this particular example, one for each of the tag paths. The
first one is for the initial path that leads into
the loop, the next one is for the final path that
leads out of the loop, and conditions three and four
are for the two paths that go around the loop. You
can verify for yourself that these conditions indeed
hold. For example, in the first one, if we assume
that the expression on the left is the hypothesis,
then we can use that to substitute in the expression
on the right to show that it is true. When $A = X$,
$Y = B$, and $Y > 0$; substituting into the right-hand
side, we find that we have
$$1 * A^B = A^B$$
which is true. In a similar manner, you can prove

that the other three hypotheses are true.   This
constitutes a proof of the correctness of this program.

          VERIFICATION CONDITIONS:

   1. $(X=A \wedge Y=B \wedge Y \geq 0) \supset (1*X^Y=A^B \wedge Y \geq 0)$

   2. $(Z*X^Y=A^B \wedge Y \geq 0) \supset [Y=0 \supset (Z=A^B)]$

   3. $(Z*X^Y=A^B \wedge Y \geq 0) \supset$
         $\left\{ Y \neq 0 \supset [Y \text{ not odd} \supset (Z*X^{2(Y \div 2)}=A^B \wedge Y \div 2 \geq 0)] \right\}$

   4. $(Z*X^Y=A^B \wedge Y \geq 0) \supset$
         $\left\{ Y \neq 0 \supset [Y \text{ odd} \supset (Z*X^{2(Y \div 2)+1}=A^B \wedge Y \div 2 \geq 0)] \right\}$

                        Figure 5

        In Figure 6, we show how to verify particular
tag paths.   In this case, we chose the path around
the loop that includes the statement Z←Z*X.   This is
the tagged path that begins with the inductive predicate, goes around the loop, and ends with the same
inductive predicate.   With loops, the initial tag
and the final tag for the path are the same assertion.   The process of verifying this path consists
of taking the given predicate and systematically
transforming it to reflect what the executable
statements in the program do to the variables.   For
example, take the inductive predicate rewritten
below the statement X←X*X and transform it backwards through the flow of the program.   What must
be true before we execute the statement X←X*X, in
order to assure that the predicate is true after we

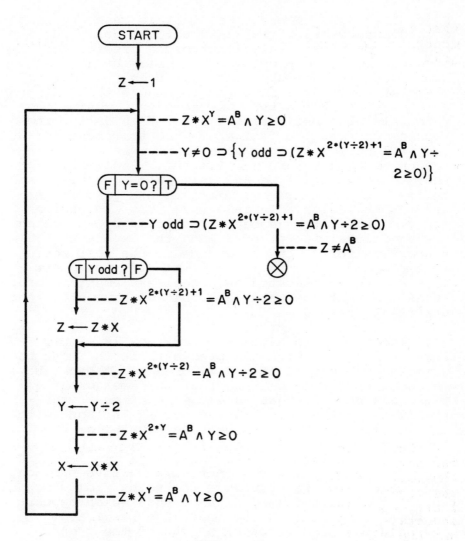

Figure 6

Derivation of Verification Condition

execute the statement? If we have an assignment statement, we simply take the expression on the right-hand side and substitute in the predicate for all occurrences of the variable on the left-hand

side of the assignment. So, in this case, we take
X^2 and substitute it in the predicate for all
occurrences of X. This transformed predicate
appears above the program statement. Using the
same rule, we ask what must have been true before
the statement $Y \leftarrow Y \div 2$ in order to assure that this
predicate is true after the statement. Using the
same rule of substituting $Y \div 2$ for Y we derive the
expression that you find above the statement $Y \leftarrow Y \div 2$.
You will notice in this case there were two occur-
rences of Y that were substituted. Similarly, for
the statement $Z \leftarrow Z * X$ we ask what must have been true
before the statement was executed and perform the
same substitution. In this case, the expression
for the predicate has been simplified by absorbing
the additional factor of X into the exponent
expression for X. When we come to the test box,
we apply the same question: What must have been
true before we executed this test statement in order
to assure that the predicate that we have after this
statement is true?

The predicate after the test box is simply
rewritten above, with the predicate in the test box
written in front of it. Now, when we go back above
the next test box, we find that we came down the
false branch. We must take the negation of the
predicate in the test box and put it in front with
an "implies" of the predicate we have below the
test box.

By transforming the initial inductive predicate
around the loop we return to the point from which
we started, with a *derived predicate* which appears
in the figure beneath the inductive predicate. We
now have two predicates on a path of the program
which are not separated by any executable statements. The two predicates apply to the same uni-
verse of variables because there are no dynamic
properties of the programs involved. The last step
is to show that the derived predicate follows
logically from the inductive predicate. This is the
formal step accomplished by the theorem prover.

The manner of derivation of the inductive

predicate assures us that the next predicate below
it is true, and the way we derived that one assures
us that the one below that is true, and so forth
down to our original inductive predicate. Thus, if
the initial inductive predicate was true and the
loop is executed, the inductive predicate will still
be true.

　　　This is the second basic principle that this
method is based on. The first is breaking the program into a fixed number of paths based on the
inductive predicate, and the second is using these
simple transformation rules based on the semantics
of the programming language, to derive transformed
predicates to prove that each path is correct.

　　　The rules we used for transforming the predicate
around the loop to derive the verification condition,
in the last example are given more explicitly in
Figure 7. These rules are for transforming the
predicates as we move backwards through the program.
Taking the assertion and moving in the reverse flow
of control of the program we derive new assertions
until we reach the point where we find the.initial
assertion of that tag path. You will notice that
there are three basic parts in this figure. One
for the typical assignment statement, one for the
test box, and one for the join of control. These
are the three basic structures used in this flow
charting or programming language.

　　　In a sense, the transformations that are performed on the predicate as we move them through
the program define the semantics of the programming
language or are defined by the semantics of the
programming language. Thus, they can be used to
explicitly describe the action of each statement in
the program.

　　　Let's look at I, the assignment statement.
We assume that the meaning of assignment statements
in this language is that the variable on the left,
x, is assigned some value calculated as a function
of the old value of that variable and all the other
variables, $\hat{y}$. The rule is simply to substitute in

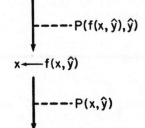

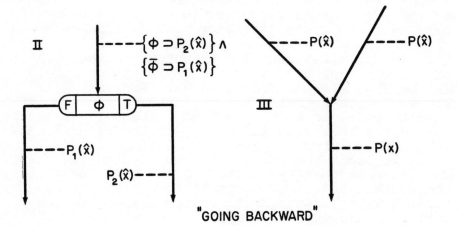

"GOING BACKWARD"

Figure 7

Semantic Definitions

$p(x,\hat{y})$ for the expression that describes and calculates the new value for x. So, in this case, we
derive $p(f(x,\hat{y}),\hat{y})$ above the assignment statement.

Now let us look at II, the text box. If we
know that after the execution of the test we want
to have $p_1(x)$ true on the false branch and $p_2(x)$
true on the true branch, then before this test is
executed
    $\{\phi \quad p_2(x)\underline{<}\}\wedge\{\overline{\phi} \quad p_1(x)\}$ must be true.

On the join of control, III, if we want to insure that p(x) is true after the join, then we must simply verify that p(x) is true on either of the branches that lead to the join.

Figure 8 shows the corresponding rules for transforming the predicates going forward. In our example, we went backwards over paths but one can, if one wishes, go forward. Then what we want to do is to say that if p(x,y) is true before we execute

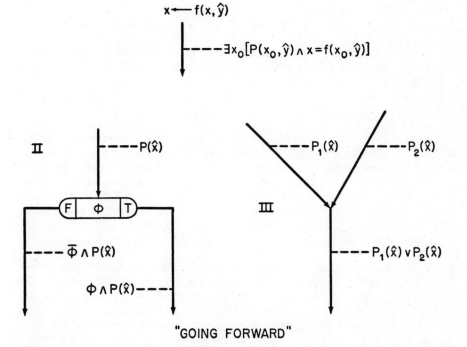

"GOING FORWARD"

Figure 8

Semantic Definitions

this type of statement, then that must be true as a consequence afterwards.

Suppose we say that $p(x,\hat{y})$ is true and we assign x a new value $f(x,\hat{y})$. Then as a consequence of those two things, there exists an x_0, equal to the "old" value of x. But, since that old value is no longer available at this point in the program, we just hypothesize that there must have been an x such that $p(x_0,\hat{y})$ is true, which is what we knew before about the value of x. Next, the new x is related to the old x_0, since the new x was calculated as a function of the old x_0, namely, $f(x_0,\hat{y})$.

Going forward on the test branch (II in the figure), if we know $p(x)$ is true before we make the test, then the test merely gathers more information for us about the predicate that is being tested.

In the third diagram, if we knew that p_1 was true on the left branch of the join and p_2 was true on the right branch of the join, then after the join we know that either p_1 or p_2 must have been true.

For other programming languages, one can make similar definitions of how to transform the predicates based on the semantics of that programming language. In fact, one can make these definitions for languages like ALGOL, FORTRAN, or PL/I, including very complicated programming concepts such as side effects, block structure, subroutines, and so forth. It is not a simple job, but it can be done.

Now, we wish to turn to another aspect of debugging, using these techniques (see Figure 9). In this case, we are concerned about the situation that one is unable to prove that his program is correct. Returning to the original example, we assume in this figure that the programmer omitted the statement "Z ← 1." Now the question is, What effect does this have on our attempt to prove that the program is correct, because, of course, now it is not correct? The assignment statement Z ← 1 is on the

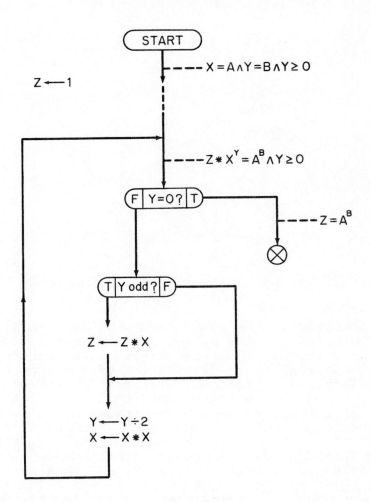

Figure 9

Forgotten Statement "Z←1"

initialization path from the initial predicate to
the inductive predicate. Let us review the proof of
that path (see Figure 10). In the previous case,

VERIFICATION CONDITION 1) BECOMES:

$$(X=A \wedge Y=B \wedge Y\geq 0) \supset (\underbrace{Z*X^Y}=A^B \wedge Y\geq 0)$$

$$\begin{array}{c} \uparrow \\ was \\ \downarrow \\ 1*X^Y \end{array}$$

TRIAL PROOF

SUBSTITUTE A for X,
B for Y:

$$Z*A^B = A^B$$

TRUE ONLY IF:

$$Z=1$$
$$\text{or } A=0$$

Figure 10

when the program was correct we had, as a verification condition, the first expression on the slide,
with $1*X^Y$ where we now have $Z*X^Y$. This is because,
in the original (correct) version of the program,
Z was initialized to one. We try to prove this
verification condition by substituting A for X and
B for Y, because these are conditions given in the
hypothesis on the left-hand side. We derive an
expression $Z*A^B = A^B$ from the right-hand side of the
expression. By examining this equation, we conclude
that it would be true if Z was 1, and thus we have
a very good clue as to what was wrong with this
program. Namely, that Z should have been 1. So,
in this simple example, we see that trying, and
failing, to prove the program was correct actually
tells us explicitly what is wrong with the program.

Let us turn to another example of an error in
this program (Figure 11). Suppose in the loop in-
stead of the statement $Z \leftarrow Z*X$, we had put $Z \leftarrow Z*Y$. In
this case, that error affects only the derivation
of the verification condition. Now, if we look at

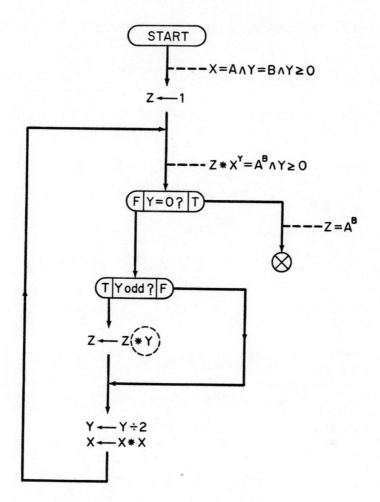

Figure 11

Put "Z←Z*Y" Instead of "Z←Z*X"

the next figure (Figure 12), we see what effect that
error has had on that verification condition. Previously we had
$$Z*Y^{2*(Y \div 2)+1}$$ and it now says $Z*Y*X^{2*(Y \div 2)}$
so that the verification condition is now different

ONLY CONDITION 4) AFFECTED BECOMES:

$$(Z*X^Y = A^B \wedge Y \geq 0) \supset \qquad \overset{\text{was } Z*X^{2*(Y\div 2)+1}}{}$$

$$\left\{ Y \neq 0 \supset \left[Y \text{ odd} \supset (\overbrace{Z*Y*X^{2*(Y\div 2)}} = A^B \wedge Y \div 2 \geq 0) \right] \right\}$$

OLD PROOF: from $Z*X^Y = A^B$, $Y > 0$, Y odd

                    show $Z*X^{2(Y\div 2)+1} = A^B$

SUBSTITUTE FOR "A^B" $Z*X^{2(Y\div 2)+1} = Z*X^Y$

                    show $2*(Y\div 2)+1 = Y$

                    when $Y > 0$, Y odd is TRUE.

NEW PROOF: .
                                .
                                .
                    $Z*Y*X^{2(Y\div 2)} = Z*X^Y$

COUNTER-EXAMPLE:
                    $Z*3*2^{2(3\div 2)} = Z*2^3$

$* \begin{cases} Y=3 \\ X=2 \end{cases}$ $12Z = 8Z$

Figure 12

from what it was before. We follow along the lines
that the proof may have taken originally. We again
use the strategy of taking the left-hand part of the
verification condition as hypothesis and use that to
substitute in the right-hand side in the effort to
derive *true*. If we try to substitute the expression
$Z*X^{2*(Y\div 2)+1}$ for A^B
we find as part of the right-hand side the equation
$Z*X^{2*(Y\div 2)+1} = X^Y$

It will be true if we can show that the two expo-
nents for X are equivalent. We attempt to show that
$2*(Y \div 2)+1=Y$. If we again return to the initial
form of the verification condition, we find two
additional hypotheses that $Y>0$ (from the fact that
it must be ≥ 0 but $\neq 0$) and that Y is odd. Under
these two conditions it is, in fact, true that
$2*(Y \div 2)+1=Y$. So, this is a sketch of how the proof
of the correct verification condition may have
transpired. Now, if we try to construct a proof
of the erroneous verification condition by doing the
same steps, we get down this time to an equation
that looks like

$$Z*Y*X^{2*(Y \div 2)}=Z*X^Y \quad .$$

You can see the difference, at this point, in the
proof because of the difference of the verification
condition.

Well, we may give up trying to prove the verification condition and try to find a counter-example
that shows that the condition is indeed not true.
In this case, we can find a counter-example when
$Y=3$ and $X=2$. We see that the expression reduces to
$12*Z=8*Z$, which is simply not true. We can use this
counter-example to the verification condition to go
back to the program and give us explicit numeric
values for which the program won't work. For
example, in Figure 13, we see that the verification
condition was generated at the point in the loop
directly above the statement "Y = 0?." That is the
point at which the verification condition was generated so that is the point in the flow in the
program to which the counter-example applies. If
we start at that point with $Y=3$ and $X=2$ and assume a
value for Z and we execute once around the loop, we
will discover that the program isn't correct, and,
in fact, once around the loop should exhibit to us
the error in the program. So, when we fail to prove
the verification condition and discover a counter-
example, then the counter-example can be used in the
program to actually give us values for which we can
execute that path, and at the end of the execution
of that path we will have an inconsistency.

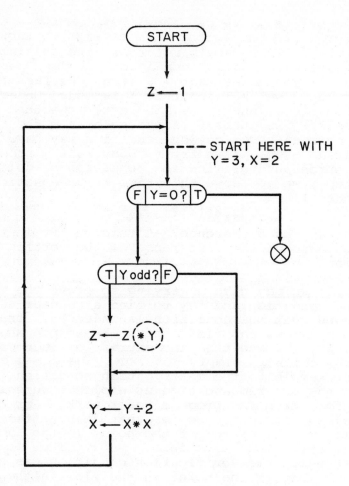

Figure 13

Apply Counter-Example to Program

In conclusion, I'd simply like to review the points that I attempted to make in this talk. First, there is a formal technique for examining programs that have been annotated with assertion predicates that allows you to prove whether the program is consistent with those predicates or not.

The method is based on two basic procedures. One, using inductive predicates, breaks the flow through the program into a fixed number of tag paths which can be used to cover any execution flow of the program. The second procedure verifies each tag path independently by showing that if the path's initial condition is satisfied, then its final condition will be satisfied. This gives a proof for any execution of the program. Then, as the final step, I tried to show how failure to prove the program can give very explicit information as to errors in the program and how that program can be corrected. The important aspect of this whole process is that you never need to run the program. If you can construct the proof that the program is correct, you will know that the program will always run correctly for any input data that satisfies the initial condition.

Proving that a program is correct can be a very costly, time-consuming, and tedious job, but when one considers the pay-off that you get for having a program that will always work correctly, it is certainly well worth any effort to do so. A great deal more work needs to be done in this area to include things like finite precision of machines, complicated programs, and how to write the assertions for programs. There are many problems, but what I hoped today to show you was that at least some work has been done in this area, and it does seem somewhat promising. I want to encourage other people to understand this work and push it forward. Thank you.

40   Jim King

REFERENCES

1. Cooper, D.C., "Program Scheme Equivalences and Second Order Logic," *Fourth Ann. Machine Intelligence Workshop,* University of Edinburgh, August 1968.

2. Good, D.I., "Toward a Man-Machine System for Proving Program Correctness," *Ph.D Thesis,* University of Wisconsin, 1970.

3. Floyd, R.W., "Assigning Meanings to Programs," *Proc. Symp. Appl. Math.,* Amer. Math. Soc., Vol. 19, 1967, 19-32.

4. ——, "The Verifying Compiler," Computer Science Research Review, *Carnegie Mellon University Annual Report,* 1967, 18-19.

5. King, J.C., "A Program Verifier," *Ph.D Thesis,* Carnegie Mellon University, September 1970.

6. ——, and R.W. Floyd, "Interpretation Oriented Theorem Prover Over Integers," *ACM Sym. of Theory of Comp.,* Northampton, Massachusetts, May 1970.

7. London, R.L., "Proof of Algorithims - A New Kind of Certification," *CACM,* Vol. 13, No. 6, June 1970, 371-373.

8. ——, "Bibliography on Proving the Correctness of Computer Programs," *Machine Intelligence 5,* Edinburgh University Press, 1970, 569-580.

9. Manna, Z., "Properties of Programs and the First-Order Predicate Calculus," *JACM,* Vol. 16, No. 2, April 1969, 244-255.

10. ——, and Pnueli, A., "Formalization of Properties of Recursively Defined Functions," *ACM Sym. on Theory of Comp.,* May 1969.

11. von Neumann, J., and Goldstine, H.H., "Planning and Coding Problems for an Electronic Computing Instrument," *Collected Works of John von Neumann,* A.H. Taub (Ed.), Pergamon Press, N.Y., 1961, 80-235.

TOP DOWN PROGAMMING IN LARGE SYSTEMS

Harlen Mills
IBM Federal Systems Division

*Structured programming can be used to develop
a large system in an evolving tree structure of
nested program modules, with no control branching
between modules except for module calls defined in
the tree structure. By limiting the size and
complexity of modules, unit debugging can be done
by systematic reading, and the modules executed
directly in the evolving system in a top down testing process.*

INTRODUCTION

Large systems programming today is dominated
by the integration and debugging problem, because
it is commonly assumed that logic errors are inevitable in programming systems (in contrast to syntax
errors which are detected by translators). There
is no doubt that programmers are fallible, and
always will be. But it now appears possible to
organize and discipline the program design and
coding process in order to 1) prevent most logic
errors in the first place, and 2) detect those
errors remaining more surely and easily than before.

We will use the term "structured programming"
to denote a complex of ideas of organization and
discipline in the programming process. There are
two major principles involved. First, beginning
with a functional specification, we will show that
it is possible to generate a sequence of intermediate systems of code and functional subspecifications so that, at every step, each system can be
verified to be correct — i.e., logically equivalent to its predecessor system. The initial system
is the functional specification for the program,
each intermediate system includes the code of its
predecessor, and the final system is the code of
the program. The transitivity of these step-by-
step equivalences then insures the correctness of
the final code with respect to the initial functional specifications. The code of the program is
generated from the "top down" in this sequence of
intermediate systems. Second, it can also be shown
that the control logic of each successive system
of code and functional subspecifications can be
completely organized in terms of a few basic control
structures, each with a single entry and a single
exit. Three basic control structures sufficient for
control logic are 1) simple sequencing,
2) IFTHENELSE, and 3) DO WHILE structures, already
known in several languages, e.g. PL/1 [9]. For
efficiency, a CASE structure may also be desirable,
e.g., as defined in PL360 [15].

The iterated expansions of functional specifications and of intermediate functional subspecifications into code and, possibly, into more detailed
functional subspecifications reflect a rigorous
step-by-step process of program design. Each
functional subspecification defined in an intermediate system represents only a mapping of initial
data into final data for some segment of coding yet
to be specified. The expansion process describes
the means selected for this mapping, using possibly
more detailed mappings to be similarly described
later.

In traditional terms, this programming design
process is carried out top down on paper, using flow

charts or any other conceptual objects available
to describe the design structure selected for each
portion of the system. Once the design is com-
pleted, the resulting modules defined are coded,
unit tested, integrated into subsystems, then into
a system, and finally debugged as a system, in a
bottom up coding and testing process.

In the structured programming process, this
design structure is carried out directly in code,
which can be at least syntax checked, and possibly
executed, with *program stubs* standing in for functional subspecifications. Instead of paper flow
charts, the structured design is defined in
IF THEN ELSE and DO WHILE code which connect newly
defined subspecifications. In fact, program stubs
can be used to simulate the estimated core and
throughput requirements of the code yet to be developed for given functional subspecifications,
during executions of intermediate systems.

The functional expansion process can be carried
out literally in a page of code at a time, in which
new functional subspecifications are denoted by
names of dummy members of a programming library,
which will eventually hold the code for the next
level of expansion. Such a page, called a *segment*,
is, itself, identified by a name and corresponding
functional subspecification at the next higher
level segment in the programming system. The
segments of a program form a tree structure.

A functional subspecification, as a mapping
from initial data to final data, has no implicit
control logic, and this is reflected in its
corresponding segment. A segment has only one
entry, at the top; and one exit, at the bottom. If
other segments are named within it, such segments
are, in turn, entered at the top, and exited out the
bottom, back into the naming segment. As such, a
named segment behaves precisely as a simple data
transformation statement (possibly quite complex,
according to its functional subspecification), without any possible side effects in program control.

The problem of proving the correctness of any expansion of a functional subspecification is thereby reduced to proving the correctness of a program of at most one page, in which there exist, possibly, various named subspecifications. The verification of the given segment requires a proof that the segment subspecification is met by the code and named subspecifications. These named subspecifications will be subsequently verified, possibly in terms of even more detailed subspecifications, until segments with nothing but code are reached and verified.

The foregoing process provides a rigorous format for an activity that all programmers do, more or less, and good programmers do well, in designing programs. But it further converts the design into code directly, and provides a vehicle for maintaining the integrity of the developing system step by step. The coding is produced "top down," rather than "bottom up," as called for by traditional standards. Integrating and control code is produced before functional code, and no unit checking of modules occurs.

SOME BACKGROUND

E. W. Dijkstra has provided several illuminating arguments for the ideas of structured programming, [2,3,4] and has exhibited a substantial application of it in the development of the T.H.E. system [5]. The critical theorem that the control logic of any program can be represented in the three basic control structures of simple sequencing, IFTHENELSE and DOWHILE structures, is due to C. Bohm and G. Jacopini [1]. The result of Bohm and Jacopini permits a new level of discipline in the programming process, which as Dijkstra also points out [4], can help reduce to practical terms the problem of proving program correctness in today's real programming systems.

There are several important developments in proving program correctness in the recent literature, which, at the very least, indicate procedures which programmers can follow in documenting and giving heuristic argumentation for the correctness of the programs they develop. Building on ideas of Floyd [6] and Naur [14], London and associates have produced formal proofs of substantial programs, themselves written for other purposes without proof methods in mind in [7, 12]; King [11] and, more recently, Good [8] have elaborated on these ideas with automatic and semiautomatic procedures for proof.

In fact, the correctness problem integrates the specification and documentation questions into programming in a natural, inevitable, and precise way. The documentation of a program should provide evidence that the program meets its functional specifications. One cannot prove a program to be correct without a definition of what it is supposed to do — its functional specification. And sufficient evidence that a program meets its functional specification can serve as its documentation.

It may appear, at the outset, that proving a system to be correct (i.e., not to depart from its original functional specifications), step by step in implementation, would be agonizingly slow and totally impractical. In fact, such an impression is no doubt behind the usual approach of coding "bottom up" from paper designs. However, when the integration and debugging activities are taken into account as well, then the step-by-step construction and verification process may turn out to be not so slow after all.

Our point of view is also very close to concepts of "functional programming," under the interpretation that functional specifications are, indeed, mathematical functions without side effects in control, and that connectives IFTHENELSE, DOWHILE, etc., are convenient forms for defining composite functions in terms of other functions.

THE IDEA OF STRUCTURED PROGRAMS

We are interested in writing programs which are highly readable, whose major structural characteristics are given in hierarchical form and are tied in closely to functional specifications and documentation. In fact, we are interested in writing programs which can be read sequentially in small segments, each under a page in length, such that each segment can be literally read from top to bottom with complete assurance that all control paths are visible in the segment under consideration.

There are two main requirements through which we can achieve this goal. The first requirement is GOTO-free code, i.e., the formulation of programs in terms of a few standard and basic control structures, such as IF-THEN-ELSE statements, DO loops, CASE statements, DECISION tables, etc., with no arbitrary jumps between these standard structures. A critical characteristic of each such control structure is that it contains exactly one entry and one exit. The second requirement is library and macro substitution facilities, so that the segments themselves can be stored under symbolic names in a library, and the programming language permits the substitution of any given segment at any point in the program by a macro-like call.

PL/I in OS/360 [10] has both the control logic structures and the library and macro facilities necessary. Assembly language in OS/360 has the library and macro facilities available, and a few standard macros can furnish the control logic structures required.

Bohm and Jacopini [1] give a theoretical basis for programming without arbitrary jumps (i.e., without GOTO or RETURN statements), using only a set of standard programming figures, such as mentioned above. We take such a possibility for granted, and note that any program, whether it be one page or a hundred pages, can be written using only IF-THEN-ELSE and DO WHILE statements for control logic.

The control logic of a program in a free form
language, such as PL/1, can be displayed typograph-
ically, by line formation and indentation conventions. A "syntax-directed program listing" — a
formal description for such a set of conventions —
is given by Mills in [13]. Conventions often are
used to indent the body of a DO-END block, such as

```
DO I=J TO K;

    statement 1
    statement 2
    ...
    statement n

END;
```

and clauses of IF-THEN-ELSE statements such as

```
IF X > 1 THEN

    statement 1

ELSE

    statement 2  .
```

In the latter case, if the statements are themselves
DO-END blocks, the DO, END are indented one level,
and the statements inside them indented further, such
as

```
IF X > 1 THEN
    DO;
        statement 1
        statement 2
        ...
        statement k
    END;
ELSE
    DO;
        statement k + 1
        ...
        statement n
    END;
```

In general, DO-END and IF-THEN-ELSE can be nested
in each other indefinitely in this way.

SEGMENT-STRUCTURED PROGRAMS

Since it may not be obvious, at the outset, how
a structured program can be developed, we begin with
a more conventional approach. Suppose any large
program has been written in PL/I — say several thousand lines of code — by any means of design and
coding available. The theorem of Bohm and Jacopini
[1] is proved constructively, so that it is possible,
mechanically, to transform the program we have in
mind into a GO TO-free program. Ordinarily, using
programming insight, this can be done with little
loss of efficiency. Now, we are in a position to
imagine a hundred page PL/I program already written
in GO TO-free code. Although it is highly structured,
such a program is still not very readable. The
extent of a major DO loop may be 50 or 60 pages, or
an IF-THEN-ELSE statement take up ten or fifteen
pages. There is simply more than the eye can com-
fortably take in or the mind retain for the purpose
of programming.

However, with our imaginary program in this
structured form, we can begin a process which we
can repeat over and over until we get the whole program defined. This process is to formulate a one-
page skeleton program which represents that hundred-
page program. We do this by selecting some of the
most important lines of code in the original program and then filling in what lies between those
lines by names. Each new name will refer to a new
segment to be stored in a library and called by a
macro facility. In this way, we produce a program
segment with something under 50 lines, so that it
will fit on one page. This program segment will be
a mixture of control statements and macro calls with
possibly a few initializing, file, or assignment
statements as well.

The programmer must use a sense of proportion

and importance in identifying what is the forest and
what are the trees out of this hundred-page program.
It corresponds to writing the "high level flow chart"
for the whole program, except that a completely
rigorous program segment is written here. A key
aspect of any segment referred to by name is that
its control should enter at the top and exit at the
bottom, and have no other means of entry or exit
from other parts of the program. Thus, when reading a segment name, at any point, the reader can be
assured that control will pass through that segment
and not otherwise affect the control logic on the
page he is reading.

In order to satisfy the segment entry/exit requirement, we need only to be sure to include all
matching control logic statements on a page. For
example, the END to any DO, and the ELSE to any IF
THEN should be put in the same segment.

For the sake of illustration, this first segment
may consist of some 20 control logic statements, such
as DO-WHILE's, IF-THEN-ELSE's, perhaps another 10 key
initializing statements, and some 10 macro calls.
These 10 macro calls may involve something like 10
pages of programming each, although there may be
considerable variety among their sizes.

Now we can repeat this process for each of
these 10 segments. Again, we want to pick out some
40 to 50 control statements, segment names, etc.,
which best describe the overall character of that
program segment, and to relegate further details to
the next level of segments. We continue to repeat
the process until we have accounted for all the code
in the original program. Our end result is a program, of any original size whatsoever, which has been
organized into a set of named member segments, each
of which can be read from top to bottom without any
side effects in control logic, other than what is
on that particular page. A programmer can access
any level of information about the program, from
highly summarized data at the upper-level segments
to complete details in the lower levels.

In our illustration, this one-hundred-page program may expand into some hundred and fifty separate segments, because 1) the segment names take up a certain amount of space, and 2) the segments, if kept to a page maximum, may average only some two-thirds full on each page. Each page should represent some natural unit of the program, and it may be natural to only fill up half a page in some instances.

CREATING STRUCTURED PROGRAMS

In the preceding section, we assumed that a large-size program somehow existed, already written with structured control logic, and discussed how we could conceptually reorganize the program into a set of more readable segments. In this section, we observe how we can create such structured programs a segment at a time in a natural way. It is evident that program segments as we have defined them are natural units of documentation and specification, and we will describe a process which develops code, subspecifications and documentation, concurrently. First we note that a functional specification corresponds to the mathematical idea of a function. It is a mapping of inputs into outputs, without regard as to how that mapping may be accomplished. Each segment defined in the preceding development represents a transformation on data, namely, a mapping of certain initial values into final values. In fact, intermediate values may be created in data as well. Corresponding to this mapping of initial into final data is a subspecification which ordinarily will be deduced directly out of the specification for the naming segment. It represents part of the work to be done in the segment. The entire page of code and new segment names must produce precisely the mapping required by the functional specification of that naming segment.

When all segments named have been assigned functional specifications, then the logical action of that naming segment can be deduced from the code

and those named specifications. Methods of proving
the correctness of programs can be applied to this
single page. The specifications may be too complex
to carry out a completely rigorous proof of correctness, but at the very least, there is on one page
a logical description of a function which can be
heuristically compared with the functional specification for that segment. The argumentation that
the function does, indeed, duplicate the functional
specification for that segment is the documentation
for that segment.

Our main point is to observe that the process
of coding can take place in practically the same
order as the process of extracting code from our
imaginary large program in the previous section.
That is, armed with a program design, one can write
the first segment which serves as a skeleton for the
whole program, using segment names where appropriate to refer to code that will be written later.
In fact, by simply taking the precaution of insert-
ing dummy members into a library with those segment
names, one can compile or assemble, and even
possibly execute, this skeleton program, while the
remaining coding is continued. Very often it makes
sense to put a temporary write statement, "got to
here OK," as a single executable statement in such
a dummy member. More elaborately, a dummy member
can be used to allocate core and to simulate processing time required, during executions of the intermediate system containing it.

Now the segments at the next level can be
written in the same way, referring as appropriate
to segments to be later written (also setting up
dummy segments as they are named in the library).
As each dummy segment becomes filled in with its
code in the library, the recompilation of the segment that includes it will automatically produce
updated, expanded versions of the developing program. Problems of syntax and control logic will
usually be isolated within the new segments so that
debugging and checkout go correspondingly well with
such problems so isolated.

It is clear that the programmer's creativity
and sense of proportion can play a large part in
the efficiency of this programming process. The
code that goes into earlier sections should be
dictated, to some extent, not only by general
matters of importance, but also by the question of
getting executable segments reasonably early in the
coding process. For example, if the control logic
of a skeleton module depends on certain control
variables, their declarations and manipulations may
need to be created at fairly high levels in the
hierarchy. In this way, the control logic of the
skeleton can be executed and debugged, even in the
still skeleton program.

Note that several programmers may be engaged
in the foregoing activity concurrently. Once the
initial skeleton program is written, each programmer
could take on a separate segment and work independently within the structure of an overall program
design. The hierarchical structure of the programs
contribute to a clean interface between programmers.
At any point in the programming, the segments
already in existence give a precise and concise
framework for fitting in the rest of the work to
be done.

FUNCTION DESCRIPTION AND EXPANSION

We have noted above that the structured programming process represents a step-by-step expansion of
a mathematical function into simpler mathematical
functions, using such control structures as
IFTHENELSE and DOWHILE. Ordinarily, we think of
this expansion in terms of a page of code at a time.
However, we can break that expansion down to much
more elementary steps, namely, into a single control
structure at a time. In this case, we ask the
question, "What elementary program statement can be
used to expand the function?" The expansion chosen
will imply one or more subsequent functional specifications, which arise out of the original specification. These new functional specifications can

each be treated exactly as the original functional specification and the same questions posed about them.

As a result, the top down programming process is an expansion of functional specifications to simpler and simpler functions until, finally, statements of the programming language itself are reached. Part of such a process is shown below, expanding the functional specification, "Add member to library." Such a functional specification will require more description, but the breakout into subfunctions by means of programming statements can be accomplished as indicated here.

In the example, the single letters identifying function names will be multi-character library names and the small quoted phrases may be very substantial descriptions of logical conditions or processes.

Specification (Level 0)

    f = "Add member to library"

        f expands to: g THEN h

Subspecifications (Level 1)

    g = "Update library index"
    h = "Add member text to library text"

        g expands to: IF p THEN i ELSE j

Subspecifications (Level 2)

    p = "Member name is in index"
    i = "Update text pointer"
    j = "Add name and text pointer to index"

Restatement of two levels of expansion

    f = IF "Member name is in index" THEN
        "Update text pointer" ELSE
        "Add name and text pointer to index"
        "Add member text to library text"

REFERENCES

1. Bohm, Corrado and Jacopini, Giuseppe, "Flow diagrams, turing machines and languages with only two formation rules," *Comm. ACM* 9 (1966) 366-371.

2. Dijkstra, E.W., "A constructive approach to the problem of program correctness," *BIT*, 8, No. 3 (1968) 174-186.

3. ——, *Notes on Structured Programming,* Technische Hogeschool Eindhoven, 1969.

4. ——, "Structured programming, in software engineering techniques, Burton, J.M. and Randell, B. (Eds.) NATO Science Committee (1969) 88-93.

5. ——, "The structure of the "THE" multiprogramming system, *Comm. ACM* 11 (1968) 341-346.

6. Floyd, R.W., "Assigning meanings to programs," *Proc. Symp. in App. Math.*, 19, J.T. Schwartz (Ed.), Amer. Math. Soc., Providence, R.I. (1967) 19-32.

7. Good, D.I. & London, R.L., "Computer interval arithmetic: Definition and proof of correct implementation,"

8. Good, D.I., "Toward the realization of a program proving system," *Ph.D. Thesis*, to be submitted to the University of Wisconsin, 1970.

9. *IBM System/360 Operating System: PL/1(F) Language Reference Manual,* Form C28,8201.

10. *IBM System/360 Operating System: Concepts and Facilities,* Form GC28-6535.

11. King, J.C., "A program verifier," *Ph.D. Thesis,* Carnegie Mellon University, 1969.

12. London, R.L., "Certification of algorithm 245 Treesort 3: Proof of algorithms — a new kind

of certification," *Comm. ACM* 13 (1970) 371-373.

13. Mills, H.D., "Syntax-directed documentation for PL360." *Comm. ACM* 13 (1970) 216-222.

14. Naur, P., "Proof of algorithms by general snap-shots," *BIT* 6 (1966) 310-316.

15. Wirth, N., "PL360, a programming language for the 360 computers," *J. ACM* 15 (1968) 37-74.

CRITERIA FOR A DEBUGGING LANGUAGE

Ralph Grishman
Courant Institute of Mathematical Sciences
New York University

The features of a good debugging system language are described and compared with the language of current systems. The efficiency and capabilities of various possible implementations of an interactive debugging system are explored. The characteristics of the author's debugging system, AIDS, are outlined, and the record of a session in which AIDS is used to debug a small program is presented.

Before describing the debugging system I have been working on for the past three years, I would like to discuss briefly the two basic problems which face the developer of a debugging system for a higher-level language: the design of a debugging language (i.e., user interface) and the choice of implementation.

I would suggest that a good debugging language include:

1. an "ON" or "WHEN" statement which specifies what occurrences in the user's program are to initiate debugging actions.

2.   a debugging procedure, which follows each
     "ON" or "WHEN" statement, and specifies
     what actions (such as tests of variables
     or print outs) are to be performed. The
     debugging procedure should be written in
     an easily learned restricted subset of
     the source language of the program being
     debugged.

3.   statements to invoke facilities in the de-
     bugging system not available in the source
     language.

     I would like to emphasize particularly that
the debugging language should be similar to the
source language. Since the data structures involved
are those of the source language, it is only natural
to use statements from the source language in debugging, rather than to try to put together a new
language which reflects the data structures of many
languages. Also, the resistance of most users
toward learning a new language in order to debug
their programs is not to be underestimated; a language with which they are already partly familiar
helps to overcome this resistance.

     Let's see how well a few of the current debug-
ging facilities meet these criteria. Clearly, these
specifications are most easily met by a batch-
system compiler with some debugging features added,
since the ability to write debugging procedures in
the source languages comes "for free." A few
examples are:

1.   PL/1,[1] whose "ON" statements permit checking
     for a variety of conditions including stores
     to variables, transfer of control to labels,
     and several error conditions. When one of
     these conditions occurs, a system message
     can be printed or a user-written procedure
     executed.

2.   the CODASYL proposal for debugging facilities
     in COBOL,[2] which includes facilities quite
     similar to those in PL/1. An additional

feature of interest is the variable "DEBUG-
ITEM," which can be referenced only in debugging procedures, and which contains
information about the condition which invoked
this procedure (e.g., what number line in
the program was being executed, which variable
caused this "trip," what its value was).

3.   IBM/360 FORTRAN G,[3] whose "AT" statement
      permits debugging procedures to be executed
      at specified points in the program. It is
      also possible to trace stores to variables
      but not to initiate debugging procedures as
      a result of stores (in contrast to the two
      preceding systems).

Although the full range of facilities, such as exist
in PL/1, are not available in any interactive debugging system, there are nevertheless systems of
interest:

1.   the interactive assembler-debugger developed
      for the SDS 930 at Berkeley,[4] which adds to
      a simple assembly language debugging system
      the full capabilities of an on-line macro-
      assembler, so that fairly complicated tests
      and conditional breakpoints can be quite
      easily invoked.

2.   PCS under TSS/360,[5] which, like FORTRAN G,
      has an "AT" command, but no facility for
      "tapping" on stores to variables. The "AT"
      command may be followed by a variety of
      FORTRAN-like statements, such as "IF,"
      "SET," "DISPLAY," and "BRANCH." From the
      point of view of FORTRAN users, however,
      these statements would not really fulfill
      the second criterion given above, since
      the syntax of each differs in several ways
      from that of the equivalent FORTRAN state-
      ment. In defense of TSS, I should note
      that PCS was not designed just for FORTRAN
      users.

DEBUGGING SYSTEMS: IMPLEMENTATION

To discuss the trade-offs in the implementation
of a debugging system, I have constructed a chart
(Figure 1) including, I believe, all the basic types
of implementations. These divide into two groups:
systems running directly from the source language
and systems running from the (compiled) object code.
For the latter, a "helpful" compiler — at the least,
one which writes out symbol table information on a
separate file — is highly desirable.

Within each group is a continuum of possible
implementations. Among systems running from the
source code, the variation is in the degree to which
code is executed in-line: at one extreme, pure
interpretation (such as QUIKTRAN[6]); at the other,
a compiler which generates a check on some sort of
trap signal at the beginning of each statement and
before each store. Among systems running from the
object code, the checks for program conditions
being trapped can be made by hardware, by firmware,
or by software machine simulator.   Incidentally, I
am not aware of any firmware system — that is, of
a microprogram modified to check loads, stores,
and transfers, against a table set up by a debugging
system — although this would seem a rather simple
project, especially with the variable microprogram
machines now available.

In comparing implementations, I shall be
interested primarily in conversational systems,
although some of the comments will also apply to
batch systems. I will assume that all the systems
meet two basic requirements: first, that inter-
action with the user is in the terms of the source
program (its symbols and data types), and second,
that "traps" on loads and stores can be turned on
and off during a debugging session (in the case of
systems using the object code, that these traps need
not be specified at compile time).   The second requirement implies that in a "compile with tests"
implementation, a test for a "trap" must be made
before *every* load and store.

	Catch Compiler and Assembly Language Errors?	Efficiency	Language Specific Tests	Modifications
Run Directly From Source Interpret	No	Fair	Good	Easy
Compile with Tests		Good		Moderately Difficult
Run From Object Code Instructions Checked By: Hardware	Yes	Good	Poor	Difficult
Firmware				
Software		Poor		

Figure 1

Comparison of Debugging System Implementations

I have included four points of comparison in the chart (Figure 1):

1. Can the debugging system find errors introduced by the standard compiler, or in assembly language routines (including operating system routines)? Clearly, systems which run directly from the source code, and hence provide their own language processor, cannot, while systems running from the object code will do so without any extra effort.

2. How efficient is the system (relative to normal program execution)?

3. How easily can language-specific checks be made? (For example, agreement in type of

formal and actual subroutine parameters
in FORTRAN.) In many cases, systems running from the object code can only make
such checks with the assistance of a
cooperative compiler.

4.   How easily can modifications be made during
      a debugging session? In particular, can
      symbol declarations (type or dimension
      statements) be changed without having to
      reprocess the entire source program?
      Source program interpreters generally keep
      such information in tables so that it can
      be easily changed. A "compile with tests"
      system may refer to tables for dimension
      information, but will compile arithmetic
      operations in-line, so that changing the
      type of a variable will most likely
      necessitate a recompilation. In object
      code systems, any change in a symbol's
      attributes will probably require recom-
      pilation.

       I should remark here that the characteristics
of an object code debugging system are in many ways
a function of the compiler used to generate the
code. At one extreme, a highly optimizing compiler
may entirely rearrange the operations in a program;
debugging a program thus compiled with an object
code debugging system may be a rather confusing
experience. At the other extreme, statements may
be compiled independently, without optimization. If,
in addition, the compiler places some signal in the
compiled code to mark the start of a new statement,
as Gaines has suggested,[7] the object code system
can offer execution on a statement-by-statement,
rather than an instruction-by-instruction, basis.
Under these circumstances, the chief disadvantage
of an object code over a source code debugging
system would be that some modifications (e.g., to
declarations) would require recompilation.

       One other interesting observation which can be
made is the effect on an object code system of a
machine oriented toward a high-level language. In

this case language-specific tests can be made easily,
and modifying the program will be simpler (although
an optimizing compiler will still cause some
difficulty). If memory references and branches can
be trapped by the hardware, no code interpretation
is necessary, so the debugging system will be
efficient as well. Despite the advantages, at least
in principle, of such a machine design for debugging,
the only commercial machine I know which meets these
specifications is the Burroughs 5500 (and the other,
similar machines in the Burroughs series).[8]

What conclusions can be drawn from this chart?
Assuming for the moment that we have a machine with
a conventional architecture, which user will prefer
which system implementation? The user who codes
in a single high-level language and doesn't want to
know any more about the system than he has to will
probably be happiest with a source language interpreter, since he can then work entirely in terms of
his source program, and modify his program without
restriction. If the program runs too long to be
interpreted, a compile-with-tests implementation
may be suitable. On the other hand, people who
have to find bugs in assembly language routines
(their own or those of the operating system) or
errors introduced by the compiler need an object
code system.

AIDS was intended for use by system programmers
and users with both FORTRAN and assembly language
routines, so an object code system was chosen.
Since the Control Data 6600 has no special provisions
for trapping loads, stores, or branches, a machine
simulator was written to monitor the user's program.

AIDS: COMMAND LANGUAGE

Before presenting a sample AIDS debugging run,
I will give an overview of the AIDS command language. Figure 2 shows the overall flow of data in
a debugging run. One starts with a source program
which one submits to an unmodified FORTRAN compiler

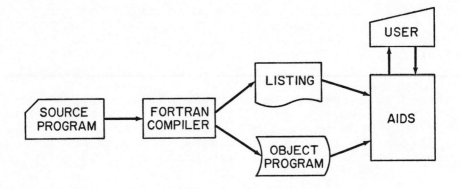

Figure 1

Data Flow in an Aids Debugging Run

or assembler. The compiler (or assembler) generates
an object program and a listing. AIDS first reads
through the listing, extracting the attributes
(address, dimensions, type) of all symbols (variable
names, statement numbers, common block names, entry
points). AIDS then loads the user's program and
asks the user, at the teletype, what he would like
to do.

The AIDS debugging language has three basic
syntactic entities: the *tag,* the *expression,* and
the *event.*

The tag specifies a word or block of words in
memory. It can be a variable name, a statement
number (indicated by a suffix 'S'), an entry point
name (indicated by a prefix '$'), an assembly lan-
guage tag, or an octal address. Symbols in a subroutine are designated by $ subroutine-name after
the symbol. An array name may appear with or with-
outsubscripts; without them, the name specifies
the entire array.

```
TAG ex.:

        VARBLE
        200S
        VARBLE $ SUBR
        $ ENTRYPT
```

The expression specifies a value, and has the same rules as in FORTRAN IV, except that function references are excluded. Full mixed mode, with logical, relational, and arithmetic operators, is allowed. In addition, one can refer to hardware registers (X1, B1, P) and some special values (such as SQ, the last quantity stored by the program) just like variables.

```
EXPRESSION ex.:

    (DP * 3.DO) ** 2
    (I. AND. 40000B). EQ. 0
    (P. GE. 420B). AND. (P. LE. 440B)
```

The event specifies an occurrence in the user's program. There are currently five types of events in AIDS: execution of a particular *opcode*, execution of the instruction *at* a particular location, a *load* or *store* to a particular location, or a *call* to a particular location. An example of each is shown below. Note that if Q is an array name, "LOADS FROM Q" specifies a load from any element of Q.

```
EVENT ex.:

          OPCODES 4 TO 7
          AT 50S
          LOADS FROM Q
          STORES TO (F,G)
          CALL $ EXIT
```

The *trap statement* is the principal statement
in the AIDS debugging language. It says that
immediately BEFORE or AFTER (WHEN is synonymous
with BEFORE) a specified event, a specified sequence
of AIDS commands is to be executed. The TRACE
statement is a special form of trap statement; it
requests that each time the event occurs, AIDS print
out a one-line description of the event. the IGNORE
statement turns off all traps on an event.

```
TRAP STATEMENT

    {WHEN   }
    {BEFORE}   event, trap sequence
    {AFTER }
     TRACE event
     IGNORE event
```

The trap sequence is a series of AIDS commands,
separated by commas. Nine different commands are
allowed in a trap sequence:

```
COMMANDS IN TRAP SEQUENCE

    variable = expression
    IF (expression)
    GO TO tag
```

```
SUSPEND trap type
RESUME trap type
PRINT "text," tag
SNAP
TRACE
PAUSE
```

The first three are the familiar FORTRAN assignment,
IF and GO TO statements. SUSPEND and RESUME turn
off and on all traps of a given class (opcode, load,
store, etc.). PRINT prints the text in quotes or
the contents of a variable. SNAP gives a "snap-
shot dump" of the registers, TRACE prints a one-line
description of the event which caused the trap, and
PAUSE causes AIDS to ask the user, at the teletype,
what he would like to do next.

   The AIDS debug language includes quite a few
other commands; four of the more interesting ones
are:

```
SOME OTHER COMMANDS

    STEP n
    RETREAT n
    BREAK OUT AT tag
    BREAK IN AT tag
```

STEP n tells AIDS to execute the next n instructions
and then pause. RETREAT n asks AIDS to restore the
user's program to the status it had prior to the
execution of the last n instructions; both registers
and memory are restored to their previous values.
(Each time the user's program performs a store, AIDS
saves the previous contents of that location in a
circular buffer; twice during each circuit of this
buffer, the simulated hardware registers are saved.
When a RETREAT is requested, AIDS 1) resets the
simulated registers to their previously saved values;
2) restores memory by working backwards through the
circular buffer from the present position to the
point where the registers were saved. The RETREAT
is generally limited by the buffer size to a few
thousand instructions, but this usually proves
sufficient.

The BREAK OUT and BREAK IN commands tell AIDS to change from simulation to direct execution, and from execution back to simulation, at the specified addresses. (BREAK IN stores a breakpoint at the location; it is the only command which alters a user's program.) If a user can localize the bug in his program, he may be able to execute most of the program directly, and only simulate a few routines. In this way the efficiency of an object code debugging system like AIDS can be greatly increased.

AIDS: A Sample Debugging Run

Consider the following program, which we are going to try to debug under AIDS:

```
      PROGRAM BUGS (OUTPUT)
      DIMENSION N (20)
    1 DO 10 K = 1, 20
   10 N(K) = 10 - K
   11 DO 20 I = 1, 10
      IP1 = I + 1
      DO 20 J = IP1, 10
      IF ( N(I) .LE. N(J) ) GO TO 20
      ITEMP = N(I)
      N(I) = N(J)
      N(I) = ITEMP
   20 CONTINUE
   30 PRINT 40, ( N(I), I = 1, 10 )
   40 FORMAT (1X, 10I2)
      STOP
      END
```

This program is supposed to perform an exchange sort of the first ten elements of N. The first DO loop, statements 1 and 10, initializes N to 9, 8, 7, 6, ..., -10. The nested DO loops over the indices I and J (statements 11 through 20) are then supposed to sort $N(1)$ through $N(10)$ into ascending sequence. Effectively, the exchange sort compares each pair of elements, and interchanges them if the larger number precedes the smaller; the three statements before statement 20 (are supposed to) perform the interchange. Finally, the first ten elements are printed out.

We compile this program, leaving the object program on LGO and the compiler listing on LISTING (AIDS will read through the compiler listing to determine the names and addresses of variables, etc.). Then, to run AIDS under INTERCOM, we type at the teletype:

COMMAND - aids (input, output, listing)	(our input is in lower case, output is in upper case)
LISTING PROCESSED	AIDS reads through listing
TYPE PROGRAM NAME - lgo	we enter name of file containing object program
PROGRAM LOADED	AIDS loads the program off LGO
BEHEST - go	AIDS asks us for our first command with "BEHEST-"; we want to try the program once, so we type "go" to start simulation
9 8 7 6 5 4 3 2 1 0	program prints out N(1) through N(10): they contain the values to which they were initialized, so the sort did absolutely nothing.

PROGRAM END

BEHEST - when stores to (i,ip1, j, n, itemp) if ($p .gt. = 11s) trace	in order to find out what's going on, we shall trace all the stores after the array is initialized (we are quite sure the initialization is working), so we tell AIDS that whenever a store is made to one of the variables listed, if p (the

	instruction location counter) is greater than the address of ("=" means the address of) statement number 11, a line describing the store (a trace) should be printed
BEHEST - when store to j, pause	each time through the inner DO loop (each time a new value is stored in j) we would like AIDS to pause (print "BEHEST-" and await a response from the teletype) so that we may ponder the trace produced so far
BEHEST - go to 1s	go back to the beginning of the program (recall that statement numbers have a suffix "s" to differentiate them from integers)
BEHEST - go	start the program again
STORE TO I=1	traces produced by AIDS
STORE TO IP1=2	
STORE TO J=2	
PAUSE.	after the store to J, we pause
BEHEST - go	so far things look all right, so we go on
STORE TO ITEMP=9	
STORE TO N(1)=8	
STORE TO N(1)=9	something wrong here - the first iteration of the loop should interchange N(1) and N(2), so the 9 picked up from N(1) should be stored into N(2)
STORE TO J=3	

PAUSE.

BEHEST - before load from itemp, n(j)= itemp, go to 20s	we look at the program to see why two stores were made to N(1), and notice that the code we have to interchange N(I) and N(J) is ITEMP=N(I) N(I)=N(J) N(I)=ITEMP clearly the last statement should be N(J)=ITEMP so we note this change on the listing; to fix this bug for the moment, we ask that, just before the load from ITEMP occurs (in the statement N(I)=ITEMP), AIDS execute instead N(J)=ITEMP and jump over the old statement N(I)=ITEMP to statement number 20
BEHEST - ignore stores to (i, ipl, j, n, itemp)	hopeful that things will work better now, we turn off the store traces
BEHEST - go to 1s	go back to the beginning of the program
BEHEST - go	and try again
0 1 2 3 4 5 6 7 8 -1	it worked...almost

PROGRAM END

BEHEST - when store to n, if ($sq .lt. 0.and. $p .gt. = 11s) trace, pause	we don't want to turn on all the store traces again, because we might get hundreds of lines of traces before we reached the point where the -1 was stored; so this time we specify that AIDS should trace the store to N and pause only if $sq ("stored

	quantity"= the contents of the word just stored by the program) is negative and, as before, the program is past statement 11
BEHEST - go to 1s	start from the beginning once more
BEHEST - go	
STORE TO N(10) =-1	we get the trace for the store to N(10), as we expected
PAUSE.	
BEHEST - retreat 12	now what? we can make use of the power of AIDS to *go back* 12 instructions in the program; after this command is executed, the program is in exactly the same state it was prior to the execution of the last 12 instructions
BEHEST - trace loads	to find out where the -1 came from, we now trace all the loads which occurred in these 12 instructions
BEHEST - go	
LOAD FROM I=10	
LOAD FROM N(10)=9	
LOAD FROM I=10	
LOAD FROM J=11	
LOAD FROM N(11) =-1	aha! the -1 came from N(11); but we were supposed to be sorting just N(1) through N(10) - why did we access N(11)? J is now 11 and I is 10, but the last pair of

```
STORE TO N(10)          elements we should be comparing
=-1                     are N(9) and N(10), so - a moment's
                        reflection will reveal - the DO
                        loop on I should only go from
                        1 to 9


PAUSE.

BEHEST - after          since there is no AIDS commands
store to i, if          to directly replace a DO loop,
(i .eq. 10)             we have to be a bit more tricky:
go to 30s               we tell AIDS that, when the store
                        to I is made at the beginning of
                        the DO loop, if I is equal to 10,
                        jump around the inner DO loop to
                        the PRINT statement

BEHEST -                turn off the load trace
ignore loads

BEHEST - go to          go back to the beginning again
1s

BEHEST - go             it worked!
0 1 2 3 4 5 6
7 8 9

*PROGRAM END*

BEHEST - quit           terminate AIDS run
```

Now, having hopefully found all the bugs in
the program, we can correct the source program,
recompile, and execute it to be sure it works.

AIDS: Success or Failure?

In closing, I think I should say a few words
about how successful AIDS has been. If popularity
is any measure of success, AIDS must be judged something less than a roaring success. Only a couple
of people are using it at New York University; the

system has been distributed to over fifteen other
installations, but feedback from these installations
has been virtually nil. I can offer two possible
reasons for this lack of popularity:

First, AIDS was designed primarily for time-
sharing (although it can also be used in batch mode).
However, difficulties with a succession of time-
sharing systems have as yet made it impossible to
use AIDS as a conversational system (I have, until
now, been unable to get AIDS to *load* under the
current version of the time-sharing system). The
impetus to use AIDS is much less in batch mode,
where a user may have several hours between runs in
which to think about a bug; under such circumstances
AIDS is used almost invariably as a "last resort."

Second, AIDS is a rather complicated system;
the debug language is about as complex as FORTRAN.
I have tried to reduce the learning effort required
by making some AIDS statements similar to FORTRAN
statements; perhaps I should have gone even further
in this direction. Nonetheless, it seems inevitable
that a certain investment of time will be required
in order to use any system as powerful as AIDS
effectively. Perhaps few users feel the need
sufficiently to make that investment.

Unquestionably, a first-class user's manual
would help; it seems that, even after learning the
commands, most people need help in selecting the
appropriate command sequences to find a particular
bug. The present user's manual requires twenty-
five pages simply to describe the format and
consequences of all the AIDS commands;[9] a more
tutorial manual, a "How to Debug Programs Using
AIDS," might require one hundred and fifty pages
(and a few months of my time). Until I get around
to writing this, my chief hope is that when AIDS
goes on-line — so that a mistake in an AIDS command
costs a few seconds, not an hour — people will
become more courageous. Until then, no final verdict
on AIDS can be brought in.

REFERENCES

1. *IBM System/360 PL/1 Reference Manual*, Form C28-8201-1.

2. *Draft-2, Proposed Debugging Facilities for COBOL*, CODASYL Programming Language Committee.

3. *IBM System/360 FORTRAN IV Language*, Form C28-6515-6.

4. Lampson, Butler, "Interactive Machine Language Programming," *Proc. FJCC 1965*, 473.

5. *IBM System/360 Time Sharing System, FORTRAN Programmer's Guide*, Form C28-2025-3, 97-106.

6. Dunn, T. M., and Morrissey, J.H., "Remote Computing, an Experimental System, Part 1: External Specifications," *Proc. SJCC 1964*, 413.

7. Gaines, R. Stockton, *The Debugging of Computer Programs*, Institute for Defense Analysis, Communications Research Division Working Paper No. 266.

8. *Burroughs B5500 Information Processing System Reference Manual*. For debugging features provided by the software, see e.g. *FORTRAN For the Burroughs 5000*, Burroughs Bulletin 5000-21029, 36-37.

9. The *AIDS User's Manual* is available from the author, Computer Documentation Office, Courant Institute of Mathematical Sciences. Additional information on AIDS also appeared in "The Debugging System AIDS" in the *Proc. SJCC 1970*.

EXTENDING THE INTERACTIVE DEBUGGING SYSTEM *HELPER*

H. E. Kulsrud
Institute for Defense Analysis

Helper is a debugging system which is inter-active and extensible. Its extensibility allows for continual upgrading in its debugging capabili-ties. The structure, orientation and evaluation of the system in its operating environment are discussed.

INTRODUCTION

The interactive extensible system HELPER was created to debug programs which have been compiled previously [1]. A user communicates with HELPER using the symbols of his source program. The parts of the object program being debugged are executed by means of a simulator. Since many program errors reveal themselves only in a true running environ-ment, it is often necessary to maintain the "real environment" during debugging. In particular, it would be undesirable to recompile or reassemble parts of the user's program purely for debugging. Since worthwhile operating systems are themselves constantly undergoing change, errors may arise from incompatibilities between working programs and the modified operating system. This constant variation

suggests that any useful debugging tool be easily
changed and extended to utilize new system features
as well as new ideas in debugging.

     HELPER was designed to be used with the IDA-
CDC 6600 operating system [2].   This operating
system is a time-shared, file-oriented system with
a great deal of extensibility.   It is highly modular
and treats many normal system functions as user
programs.

     Primary communication with the system is via
the CDC 210 entry/display consoles.   A console
consists of a video screen which displays twenty
lines of fifty characters each, a cursor to show
screen position, and a keyboard with 62 characters
and 13 function keys.   The computer also has 65 K
words of fast memory and 500K words of extended
core memory (ECS).

     The HELPER system has been in operation since
March, 1969, and is used by all levels of programmers.   The paper given in [1] supplies a complete
but preliminary description of HELPER.   What is now
of interest is the extensions that have been made
and can be made to the system.

ATTRIBUTES OF HELPER

     In order to understand the possibilities that
exist for extensibility in HELPER, a brief synopsis
of the system's attributes is necessary.   Essentially, HELPER is directed to the problems of debugging at the machine language level.   It accom-
plishes complete analysis of the program by simulation of instructions and therefore runs programs at
two speeds, normal and simulated rate.   Only those
routines or parts of routines being debugged are
simulated.   Simulation slows execution 100-200
times.   HELPER is particularly pertinent to programs
written in COMPASS assembly language [3], and IMP,
a syntax-directed system programming language [4].
For want of better tools, it is used for higher-

level languages such as FORTRAN.

The user communicates with the system by means
of a simple algorithmic command language. The
arguments of this language are the symbols of the
user's own program. In order to provide symbolic
equivalence, all compilers at IDA have been modified
to store a relocatable binary version of the symbol
table following the relocatable binary program.
This modification has become extremely useful in
all areas of debugging since many debugging tools,
such as simple memory dumps, now produce their
results in symbolic terms. Information as to the
structure of the command language is always available during a debug session.

The HELPER system is basically interactive, but
it can be used in a batch manner by specifying all
commands before commencing execution. However, the
user usually communicates during execution by means
of preplanted breakpoints, conditional commands, and
utilization of an interrupt button. HELPER commands
have both dynamic and static modes; for example,
displaying of variables may occur during a run without interrupting execution at a breakpoint.

The system allows for changing the values of
variables and code and for varying the flow of the
program. Thus, it is possible to patch in correct-
ing code and discover whether this is a correct way
of eliminating an error. Flow may be changed by
simple "GO TOS," or by backing up a few steps in
order to see what is happening in a critical section
of the program.

HELPER attempts to make as few changes to the
normal program environment as possible. There is
only one instruction of the user's program changed,
namely the first instruction to be simulated. This
aspect is especially valuable for self-modifying
programs. However, due to the system overlay
mechanism, the user's storage map may be different
during debugging. To compensate, there are many
checks on array storage for items being stored out
of block.

For the parsimonious, debug runs are restartable and replayable. The status of the program at
any point can be saved, and a later debug run
started from that point. In addition, a complete
record of the user commands and function buttons is
kept and the debug session can be rerun (replayed)
without being retyped in case a new assembly of the
program has been made. Communication with lower-
level debugging tools, such as memory dumps, is
possible during a debug session.

STRUCTURE OF HELPER

The HELPER system consists of five key elements:
a simulator, a compiler, a communicator, a controller,
and a set of debugging routines. The elements are
related as depicted in the figure below.

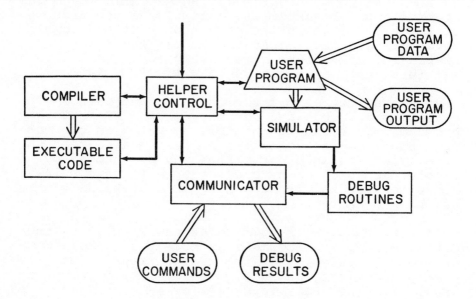

Helper Structure

The communicator is that part of the system which feeds information to the user and collects input from him. The controller organizes the traffic between the other units.

The compiler and the set of debugging routines are of interest because they provide for the extensibility of the system. The compiler is used to translate the commands given by the user. The compiler produces code incrementally and is created by a metacompiler or compiler-compiler which itself produces code incrementally [5].

The compiler accepts a line of input at a time. A line is considered to be a string of commands separated by terminators and ending with a terminator (a completely blank line or the bottom of the video screen). The commands are scanned and translated simultaneously. If there is a syntactic error, it is pointed out to the user; otherwise the resultant code is executed immediately. Some code is compiled and held for execution when certain conditions (given in the command) are met.

In order to introduce changes in the command language, only the new syntax for the compiler is fed to the metacompiler, and the resultant code replaces old code or is added on to the compiler. The throughput time to produce such changes is very short.

The debugging programs are those routines which are accessed when certain switches are set by the simulator and user commands. They carry out the actual work of finding the required information and preparing it for output. When an entirely new debugging command is introduced, the separate package is simply added to the system. If necessary, it can be checked in isolation or with the system.

COMMANDS

A HELPER command consists of an action on an address or group of addresses under the control of a count and possibly with type information. Addresses or names are specified as:

SUBR.SYMBOL↓EXP↑   EXP means expression

SYMBOL↓EXP↑   (means SYMBOL + EXP)

SUBR↓EXP↑

COMMON↓EXP↑

SUBR↓N↑   N is an octal integer
                         (SUBR + N).

COMMON↓N↑

SYMBOL↓N↑

*SYMBOL↓EXP↑   *uses the name of the sub-
                         routine currently being
                         executed.

*SYMBOL↓N↑

*N

N

AI,BI or XI   Registers.

The commands are:

START NAME,N: Start simulation at the Nth
                         execution of instruction
                         NAME.

STOP NAME,N: Stop simulation on the Nth
                         execution of instruction
                         NAME.

ON NAME:	Simulate subroutine NAME.
ON ALL:	Simulate all the user's subroutines.
OFF NAME:	Do not simulate subroutine NAME.
OFF ALL:	Do not simulate any routines.
BREAK NAME,N:	Break off execution and give the user control on the Nth execution of instruction NAME (a breakpoint).
SHOW NAME,TYPE:	Display the value of NAME in TYPE mode. TYPE can be integer, floating point, octal, BCD etc.
TRACE NAME,TYPE:	Display the value and location of NAME whenever it is used or changed, but continue execution.
TRACE SET NAME,TYPE:	Display the value and location of NAME whenever it is changed.
TRACE USE NAME,TYPE:	Display the value and location of NAME whenever it is used.
TRACE, TYPE:	Whenever a variable has no type, display it in TYPE mode.
TRACE ALL:	Display all uses of and changes to all variables.
TRACE OP N:	Display all instructions executing op code N.
TRACE FLOW:	Display all jumps which change the address counter.
GO TO NAME:	Continue execution at instruction NAME.

BACK TO NAME:	Repeat starting at the last execution of instruction NAME, restoring all variables and registers to the values they had at that time.
BACK TO -N:	Back up N instructions with variables and registers properly restored.
STEP N:	Execute and display N instructions.
STEP TO NAME:	Execute until instruction NAME and display the last ten instructions.
DUMP:	Display all registers.
DUMP NAME,N:	Display all registers on the Nth execution of instruction NAME, and continue execution.
SET NAME←EXP:	Set variable NAME to the value of expression EXP.
PATCH:	Enter the memory dump program called PATCH.

IF (EXP1 R EXP2) AT NAME,N (COMMAND:COMMAND:etc.):

If expression EXP1 has relation R (where R is =,≠,>,<,≥, or ≤,) to EXP2 on the Nth execution of NAME, execute the HELPER COMMANDS.

IF(EXP1 R EXP2)WHEN NAME,TYPE(COMMAND:COMMAND:etc.):

If expression EXP1 has relation R to EXP2 when the variable NAME is used or set, execute the COMMANDS.

HELP: Display the HELPER commands
                              currently in effect.

HELPINFO: Display the file with the
                              information explaining the
                              use of HELPER.

SAVE NAME,N: Make a restartable copy of
                              the program as it is on the
                              Nth execution of NAME.

FILE NAME: Display the file named NAME.

OUT: Display the HELPER output
                              file.

     To expand the power of these commands, some
additional symbols are also employed.

↓COMMANDS: ↓ is used for deletion of
                              commands. For example,
                              ↓STEP: discontinues the
                              stepping mode.

NAME1/NAME2/NAME3   / has the effect of causing
                              the preceding command to
                              operate on several elements.
                              For example, SHOW A/B/C: will
                              display three variables.

NAME - NAME↓EXP↑   - is used to mean inclusive.
                              Thus SHOW A - A↓10↑ displays
                              the elements A through A + 10.

INPUT/OUTPUT: Possibilities and Problems

     As has been mentioned in previous sections,
HELPER has a complicated collection of its own
input and output files. In addition to communicating
by means of the video display screen, it keeps a file
containing a record of all commands typed by the user
and the resultant output created by HELPER during the

debug run. This is the file accessed through the
command OUT. This file is accessible after the run
and can be printed so that a written record is
available.

HELPER produces a second file which contains
a record of the commands typed and the function
buttons utilized. This file is processed for replay
of the debug run. When the SAVE command is employed,
restartable copies of the program, which are also
files, are created. Furthermore, during execution
HELPER manipulates the relocatable binary files
which contain the user's programs in order to obtain
the necessary symbol tables. HELPER also fetches
any files that the user requests, for example, the
information file HELPINFO. HELPER itself consists
of many segments which are only loaded when needed
and erased subsequently in order to conserve room
in memory.

It appears that this complicated I/O structure
should be kept quite separate from the user's I/O.
A great many complications would be avoided in this
manner. However, if the obvious expedient of having
duplicate copies of I/O programs is applied, a large
increase in the memory needed would result. Aside
from the problem of having duplicate program names,
a great deal of extra effort would be required to
keep the debugging system up to date with the
evolving operating system. It would be necessary to
maintain two separate but equal I/O packages. Thus,
it seems that a compromise is in order.

This compromise results in the introduction
into HELPER of some interesting new mechanisms.
First, there is the use of level assignment. In
the IDA system, a field has been reserved for a
simple use of level numbers. All system programs
have a special level number and all user programs
have a zero level. This level number is used by
HELPER to designate which routines are to be simulated, and which run at normal speed. For example,
all system routines should be run at normal speed.
This level number also serves to differentiate
between system and user programs with the same name.

A second useful tool is the availability of a
routine for swapping common blocks used by I/O
programs. When the system is going to use the same
I/O program, it automatically interchanges the user
and system blocks so that the appropriate ones are
processed. Whenever it is possible, which is not
too often for I/O programs, reentrant code is
written. In these cases, the calling list for the
routine contains the names of the blocks to be
processed, and no swapping routine is required. A
fourth tool, useful in the case of interactive
programs, is the special HELPER command SAVE SCREEN.
This command has the effect of presenting the
correct data to the video screen and preserving the
alternate picture.

EXTENSIONS

The most important additions to the HELPER
system have come about in the area of user education.
Programmers are generally lazy about learning new
languages and forgetful of programs they have not
used for a long time. Grishman has encountered this
user inertia with his debugging system AIDS [6].
Of course, debugging systems should be made simple
enough that their features can be learned in a few
minutes, especially when those few minutes usually
occur when the user is under stress.

As can be seen from the preceding sections, a
viable debugging system is not simple. It must
operate on several levels, apply to a number of
source languages, and support various tools of
varying sophistication.

To combat the human inertia and absent-minded-
ness, the information concerning the attributes of
HELPER has been made easily accessible to the user.
As discussed in the section on commands, at any
point, the user may display the HELPINFO file.
This file is designed as a learning manual. It
contains several descriptions of the system given
in order of increasing complexity. Thus, at first,

the novice can obtain a quick one-page write-up of
the system and later can study some of the more
subtle implementation questions. The file is
indexed for finding specific items and can be key
searched in the forward and backward directions.
The initial HELPER screen display also gives a brief
review of the function buttons.

Users also tend to need reassurance that the
system is processing the commands it has been given.
Usually the user is confused about the flow of his
program but thinks it is the system that is wrong.
A few applications of the HELP command serve to
alleviate doubts of the system.

Output to the screen is scrolled. That is,
the older lines disappear off the top of the screen,
and new lines appear at the bottom of the screen.
Often the user wishes to see output more than twenty
lines ago without interrupting his run. Through use
of the OUT command he can view and key search his
output file.

As the user becomes familiar with the language
and system, his desire to avoid typing increases.
Thus, six of the function buttons have been utilized
to stand for some of the most common commands. In
addition, some joint commands have been incorporated
such as

                    START + NAME :

which means start simulating at NAME *and* execute a
breakpoint at NAME.

For lack of better tools, HELPER now aids in
the debugging of FORTRAN programs. A couple of
additions to the system were necessary in order to
handle FORTRAN more efficiently. The symbol % was
introduced to stand for blank COMMON. The notation
SUBR.N is used to specify FORTRAN statement numbers.
The FORTRAN compiler now produces a binary version
of the symbol table, and this table contains additional information for multi-dimensional arrays
with passed parameters.

Though HELPER is very flexible about modes for output, and new modes can be added without much trouble, generally communication of single word variables is made. In order to introduce complicated data types that extend over more than one word, a special subroutine feature was included in the system. When the command

    SUBR(EXP1,EXP2,....)

is given, the routine SUBR is loaded if absent and executed. SUBR is a user coded routine which manipulates multi-word output and sends it one word at a time to the HELPER display routine. This feature extends the output format and also allows the user to call a completely new program into the debug run.

Since one of the classic computing errors is that of storing data beyond the limits of an array, some effort has been made to check for this particular bug. Whenever HELPER is in control, it scans the memory map for consistency, and immediately reports the whereabouts of any destroyed blocks. Though this method is not sufficient for obtaining all errors of this type, it will find many errors, especially those of clearing too much to zero.

FUTURE EXTENSIONS

Small changes, particularly those suggested by the users, are constantly being incorporated into the HELPER system. Currently, these involve joint commands, extended data types, and more button abbreviations. More extensive revisions are being considered for the future.

Of particular importance is the problem of very, very large problems. The case of long running problems has been solved via the SAVE feature. However, there are always programs which use the entire computer memory and reveal bugs only when they have been scaled up for full production. A possible solution for these programs is to put the

entire user code in ECS memory that is currently
reserved for system swapping.

Another possible addition is the introduction
of comparison memory dumps; That is, the ability
to scan several large snapshots of the user program
and indicate which locations have changed. Though
the implementation of comparison dumps is not difficult, it involves revising the memory allocations
of the system.

Also of interest is the display of a group of
variables which have been pre-specified. In fact,
one would like to be able to indicate several such
displays and bring them up under control of a single
button and count. Though the HELPER conditional
commands give a first step in this direction, a
scheme with less typing would be desirable.

We have learned that though HELPER is not the
perfect or ultimate tool in debugging, its extensibility allows for the continual upgrading of the
debug tools at IDA. Furthermore, it provides a
means for checking out new ideas in debugging.

I would like to thank my colleagues at IDA for
using this tool and offering many helpful suggestions.

REFERENCES

1. Kulsrud, H.E., "HELPER: An Interactive Exten-
    sible Debugging System," *Second Symposium on
    Operating Systems Principles,* (1969), 105-111.

2. Cave, R.L., "User's Guide for the IDA-CRD
    Operating System," *Working Paper No. 220,* IDA-
    CRD Log No. 8735 (January 1968).

3. *Control Data COMPASS Reference Manual,*
    No. 60190900 (April 1967).

4. Irons, E.T., "Experience With an Extensible
    Language," *Comm. ACM* 13, No. 1 (1970) 31-40.

5. Kulsrud, H.E., "A General Purpose Graphic Lan-
    guage," *Comm. ACM* 11, (1968) 247-254.

6. Grishman, R., "The Debugging System AIDS,"
    Proc. of SJCC (1970) 59-64.

EXTENDABLE NON-INTERACTIVE DEBUGGING

Jim Blair
Purdue University

*The Purdue Extendable Debugging System (PEBUG)
is a general purpose debugging system which operates
under the Purdue version of the Mace operating system
on the CDC 6500. PEBUG is designed to provide
flexible debugging in either an interactive or non-
interactive mode. The basic construction of PEBUG
primitives, debugging commands, and the interface
used for extension, are described.*

I am going to try to give an overview of the
system, by briefly describing the structure, the
main features, and the basic design goals. First,
I started out to provide symbolic debugging; particularly for higher level language users such as
those programming in Fortran or Algol. Second, I
wanted to provide flexible non-interactive debugging.

PEBUG operates on the CDC 6500 at Purdue University, which is a multi-processing machine where
several jobs can be run simultaneously. These jobs
can originate from the card reader or from remote
terminals and are processed according to a scheduling algorithm. Once the job is submitted, independent of its media or submittal, there is no way for

the programmer to communicate with the job until he
gets his output listing back. Since there was a
rise of interactive terminals at Purdue, we wanted
to provide flexible interactive debugging. Thus,
we wanted to provide a system that would enable a
person to use at least a portion of the same set of
tools whether a job was interactive or non-interactive.

Finally, we wanted to have a system that would
allow extendability to the user in terms of his
source language. I think if you've been working in
this area for very long you have found that we do
not seem to be lacking in suggestions for new tools
and new extensions for debugging. You can come up
with any kind of debugging system and yet somebody
is bound to come up with another tool and another
method for checking out their specific problem. We
are continually plagued with too narrow a system, or
we just approach a certain portion of the problem.
Thus, I wanted to have something that would be
extendable in terms of source language so that a
person who writes a Fortran program can add his own
debugging aids easily, without adding complicated
interfaces to the system.

In developing the system, we started out with
certain structural goals: first, we wanted to
produce a basic system from primitives and build
this up in various levels. Obviously, this would
make the system easier to develop, but it is also
in keeping with the idea of extendability. When we
get to the final usable system, we will also have
a system of primitives on which other debugging
systems and aids can be built. I will show you
some of the features of this later. Second, since
we are approaching the idea of debugging in an
arbitrarily given programming language, it is
obvious that the best way to approach the problem
is to provide the facilities for debugging in the
original system. We should note that in construct-
ing the original operating system and the compilers,
we need to think about providing facilities that
will enable us to provide debugging aids more
easily. Several of our talks will be directed to

this area, but currently we are faced with a rash
of processors whose designers had not considered
this originally. I am addressing myself to providing debugging aids for existing software; thus we
wanted to make as few modifications to this software as possible.

The PEBUG structure on top of the primitives
has three basic components which I want to talk
about in some detail. First, there is the breakpoint interpreter which has to do with the dynamic
control of execution and debugging; second, the
command scanner which is actually the program that
does the controlling of commands that are entered
as input; third, the group of debugging subroutines.
These subroutines are the ones that actually do the
debugging processing.

I want to consider each one of these in detail
but first I would like to describe some of the work
that was done as far as the basic primitives are
concerned. To provide symbolic debugging, we have
to get hold of the symbol tables. If we take an
existing compiler, such as a Fortran compiler or
an existing assembler, this information usually is
not left around in core at execution time. (Some
of the more recently developed processors do this,
but this information usually is not available.)
We want to build directly on the compile time tables
to provide information at execution or post-execution time. Rather than trying to build a specialized symbol table in core for the processors
considered initially (the Fortran compiler and the
Compass assembler on the CDC 6500) we went into
them and found the portion of code that writes out
the symbol table and then simply inserted procedures
that write the appropriate information onto files.

The same thing was done as far as the loader
was concerned. We went into the routine which
writes out the load map on the output file and we
added code that would simply write out the load
information with the load addresses of the program
blocks, entry point addresses, and cross-reference
information. We built primitive tables on scratch

files with as little modification to the system as
possible. These scratch files are available at
execution time or post-execution time any time after
they have been written. Routines were then written
that could be used at either execution time or post-
execution time to access these files and build
tables now standardized which are in core for rapid
access and use. This is the basic procedure that
we have followed as far as the symbol tables are
concerned. We have also considered the fact that
for post-execution debugging we need to have a
recording, or a dump, of all the information about
a job at a specific point. Normally, there are
specialized dumping routines which will give you
core dumps. These will usually just throw the
information onto the output file. For the sake of
readability we implemented a few routines which
would take what I would call checkpoint dumps. On
a scratch file we write all the information about
a job that is known: the entire central memory,
field length, and all the other system information.
We can read portions of this back into central
memory during execution time or at post-execution
time. This particular facility has been used this
year by students from our systems programming
courses. They used primitives to produce symbolic
post-execution dump routines. Then by simply using
the checkpoint procedure and by accessing the
symbol tables, they read this back in appropriate
page-size hunks, and write them out in symbolic
formats. We have quite a number of model 33 tele-
typewriters as well as a Control Data 252 which is
a graphic cathode ray tube display unit. I wanted
to illustrate the advantages of using a cathode ray
tube interactively.

THE BREAKPOINT INTERPRETER

Now the breakpoint interpreter: breakpoints
are necessary for dynamic control of execution in
the program. To set a breakpoint, you save the
instructions at a given location and then plant
some kind of a jump instruction to the debugging

processor. Now, if we are going to resume execution
of the program after debugging has been performed
at a specified breakpoint, we have to execute the
instruction that was saved. The most obvious and
simple way to do this is to throw it back into the
original location and transfer control to that
location and continue. The obvious problem here
is that you have destroyed the breakpoint that you
have set. If you are in a tight loop, it becomes
difficult to use a pair of breakpoints, traveling
back and forth, requiring that the second one be
set from the first one, etc. It is almost necessary, if you want to have a non-destructive breakpoint, to somehow execute the instruction at a given
location remotely from the original location that
it was loaded into. This is why I've talked about
a breakpoint interpreter, because I've actually
designed an interpreter which is totally integrated
with the breakpoint processor.

It should be obvious that if we have to inter-
pret the instruction that we have saved from breakpoint, the same interpreter can be used for inter-
preting all the code. Thus, we have integrated this
into one breakpoint interpreter to provide the
dynamic control of execution and debugging. This
breakpoint interpreter provides no debugging on its
own; it is simply a control processor. The breakpoint interpreter has several linked list structures
built into it; it will simply check these linked
lists to see whether there is any debugging that
has been requested along a specific type. There
are currently seven of these linked lists used by
the breakpoint interpreter. We have a list for
breakpoints themselves, that is, breakpoints that
are set and control actual execution of the program.
The rest of these have to do with tracing which is
used mainly with overlay jobs. (The low trace here
can also be used in regular execution.) When you
are dealing with overlay jobs, you are dealing with
dynamic loading of the program and you cannot, from
one overlay, set a breakpoint in a second overlay
that has not yet been loaded. You have to wait
until that overlay has been loaded and then set that
breakpoint. So, we have a load trace which gives

control any time a specific overlay is loaded. The
rest are fairly self-explanatory: simple traces for
tracing every instruction, flow traces never out of
the ordinary sequence of the instruction counter,
call traces for monitor calls, and subroutine and
variable traces for storing information into a
particular variable and for any error detection.

There are two modes of execution: one is regular execution and gives control to the debugging
processor at breakpoints only; the other is interpretive execution where every instruction is interpreted, and the interpreter keeps debugging control
all the time. In the latter mode, we can perform
such things as a simple call and variable traces
because we are watching everything that is going on.
Of course, there is an obvious overhead for this
kind of thing, but switching back and forth between
these modes is quite simple.

Let me go on now and talk more about the list
structure we are using. There is an individual
pointer for each of the types of debugging that
you might possibly want to request. Each one of
these pointers may point to a condition linked to
a list of conditions under which the appropriate
routines are to be invoked (Fig. 1). If there are
no conditions, then it is simply a zero pointer.
The conditions consist of a first and a last word
address of a block of code for which a simple trace,
call trace, etc., is to be valid. In variable
traces it is a block of code for which we are
watching any stores that take place. In other
words, if something is stored in a block of code,
we essentially trace it and give control to the
appropriate processors. For the low trace, we are
talking about overlay numbers. On the CDC we
usually deal with two identifying overlay numbers.
These numbers specify which overlay is to be loaded.
The condition on the load traces simply specify
which overlay is to be loaded and control is passed
to the appropriate link processor. For each one of
the entries in the condition-linked list there is a
pointer to a processor-linked list. So, for each
condition there is an associative processor-linked

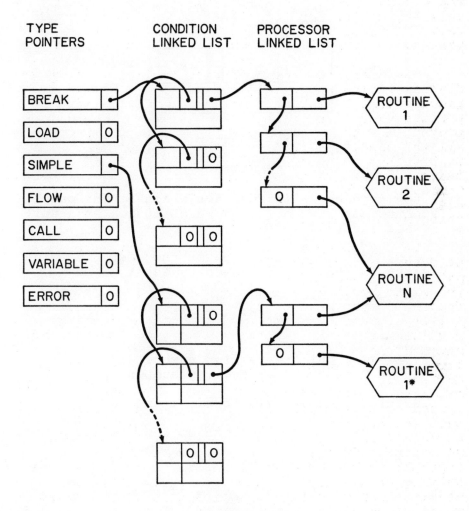

Figure 1

Breakpoint/Interpreter Linked List Structure

The *condition* linked lists of Figure 1 contain two word entries of the form:

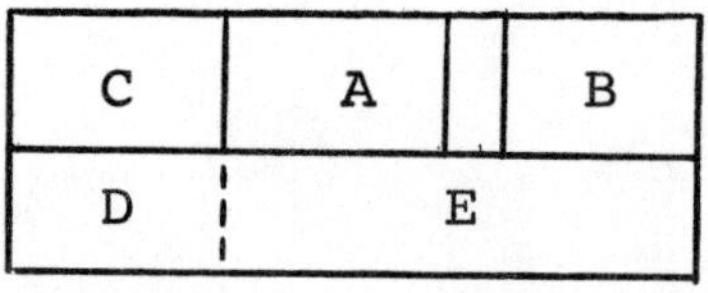

C	A	B
D		E

A is the *condition* list pointer which either points to the next entry in the list or zero, which indicates the end of the list.

B is the *processor* list pointer which either points to a processor list or zero, which indicates a null processor list.

C, D and E depend on the type of the list, in which the entry is found. If the entry is a:

> breakpoint, then
> >   C = address, DE = instruction word

> load trace, then
> >   C = primary overlay number
> >   D = secondary overlay number

> simple, flow or call trace, then
> >   C = FWA,
> >   D = LWA of instruction address block

> variable trace, then
> >   C = FWA
> >   D = LWA of effective address block

> error detection, then
> >   C = error flag

Figure 2

CONTENTS OF "CONDITION" LINKED LIST ENTRY

list which is simply a list of debugging processors
which are to be invoked in the sequence in which
they appear in the list. Thus, in this example, if
we had a simple trace which satisfied the first list
condition, routine one would be entered, this could
be any type of subroutine; when that subroutine was
finished, routine two would be entered, etc. When
routine n was finished it would return control back
to the breakpoint interpreter. The breakpoint
interpreter, in performing its interpretation, or at
a breakpoint, checks these pointers and invokes the
appropriate routines. This is a package by itself.
This is a separate primitive and it is heavily used
in PEBUG, but along with the breakpoint interpreter
are the routines which can be called to set up this
list structure. In other words, you simply set
limits which set the condition entry for a particular type of debugging and specify another routine
to set the various processes. So these routines
can be set up independently of PEBUG. Thus, they
could be used by other debugging processes. When
any one of these routines gets control at debug time,
there is certain system information passed to it that
would normally not be available, i.e., the current
instruction address, instruction word and instruction.

     This breakpoint interpreter is the central
concept as far as dynamically controlling the program
is concerned. Built onto this we have the PEBUG
system, so let us now talk about the command
scanner, the second basic ingredient of the system.

THE COMMAND SCANNER

     The command scanner is simply a processor which
will essentially process debugging requests. The
scanner is designed to be quite simple and yet
provide a flexible means for debugging. A PEBUG
command consists of a processor name and parameters
that are to be passed to that processor. Since we
are talking about a debugging situation we are
dealing mainly with addresses, either variable or

routine locations.   Thus, we have designed the parameter structure of the command scanner to deal mainly
with address quantities. Let us look at the basic
elements of which a parameter can be composed.

   (1)   Octal or decimal integers.

   (2)   Alphanumeric name. As a parameter
this is interpreted as an entry point.   It can
be either an internal entry point within the debugging system which really wouldn't be an actual
subroutine entry point, or it could be any entry
point in the system. If you want to see where a
particular subroutine was last called from, you
simply specify the name of that routine and the
system will return the first entry address of that
routine.

   (3)   An alphanumeric name followed by a slash
refers to a program block.

   (4)   An alphanumeric name (which refers to a
program block), followed by a slash and a symbol,
can be an alphanumeric name or, as in the case of
Fortran, a numeric label.

   (5)   Common blocks can be referenced by specifying the block name between slashes.

   (6)   Strings can be referenced by putting
quotes around them.

   (7)   The parameters that are passed are actually
the addresses of each elemental type. If the particular routine was expecting the value of that variable, simply add parentheses to specify its value.

   (8)   An asterisk has been used to specify a
previous parameter value. For example, in specifying a dump, the initial dump routine that was
written used a first-word and a last-word address
of the block to be dumped. But one might want to
dump the main program from location Fortran 10 and
proceed 100 words from that point; instead of
writing all this out, asterisks are used to reference

previous values.

(9)   Local names and variables were provided so that information could be stored locally in the debugging package for debugging purposes which are not stored in the program itself.   They are referenced by an alphanumeric name preceded by a dollar sign.

This is a basic structure — the PEBUG command consists of processor name followed by a list of parameters.   Parameters can be separated by either commas or blanks.   The basic parameter elements can be currently combined by addition or subtraction. In debugging, when one deals with addresses, there is not much need for multiplication and division. Any routine can be invoked by the breakpoint interpreter and by the command scanner at debug time. This is essentially the basis of future extendability.

THE COMMAND FUNCTIONS (Debugging Routines)

The debugging routines can be provided either with the particular PEBUG system loaded or by the user with his program.   Since each routine is a separate module, all the routines do not have to be loaded for any given debugging session.   Most of PEBUG's current development consists of refining and adding to these processors.

There is no direct access to the command scanner itself.   One may only use it initially to specify where the lists of commands are to be found. The scanner is used by one of several processors to process debugging commands from the appropriate input device, where each line received is passed to the scanner.

FIL is the processor which executes debugging commands from a specified file.

TRM is the processor which executes debugging

commands from a teletype.

CRT is the processor which executes debugging commands from a cathode ray tube display (interactive) terminal.

DBG is the processor which executes debugging commands stored in central memory.

If FIL reaches an end of record mark on the file or if DBG reaches the end of the command list (signified by a zero word), the command GO is automatically invoked. We shall discuss initial debugging control later.

Program execution can be resumed in one of two modes, either regular execution or interpretive execution. The mode of execution is determined by a switch ($XM). This switch can be examined and modified by appropriate debug commands, however direct modification is not necessary. There are three routines which provide the necessary processing to resume execution.

GO is the processor which resumes program execution. The execution switch ($XM) is used to determine the mode of execution.

XEQ is the processor which resumes regular execution of the program. The execution switch is set for regular execution and a GO command issued.

INT is the processor which resumes interpretive execution of the program. The execution switch is set for interpretive execution and a GO command issued.

Debugging control is obtained by either breakpoints or interpretive traps. Breakpoints and overlay load traps will regain debugging control in either mode of execution. All other interpretive traps will only regain debugging control from interpretive execution. The following processors are used to manipulate the traps and breakpoints:

AT is the processor that sets a breakpoint
at a given location. The location of the
breakpoint, the processor to be called at
this location, and any parameters to the
breakpoint processor are all specified as
parameters to the AT processor.

TRAP is the processor that sets interpretive
traps for a given block of locations. The
trap type, the location block, the processor
to be called and any parameters to that
processor are all specified as parameters
to the TRAP processor.

RMV is the processor that removes breakpoints and interpretive traps.

In debugging, even more than initial program
writing, it is sometimes quite difficult to describe
the execution paths and results of a program. Quite
often when a bug is actually encountered, we discover
that we need to examine the program state prior to
the occurrence of the problem in more detail. To
facilitate this procedure "checkpoint" dumps have
been provided. Checkpoint dumps with two identifying numbers can be taken at any time. The status
of the program's central memory at the time of a
checkpoint can be restored at a later time and
debugging continued. In general, files are not
disturbed by taking checkpoint dumps or by restoring
from checkpoint dumps; however, no attempt is
currently made to preserve the position of files.
Since general file allocation and positioning is
quite diverse and difficult to automatically repro-
duce, file positioning is currently the responsi-
bility of the user.

CKP is the processor which causes a
checkpoint dump to be taken.

RES is the processor which restores a
program to the status at a given checkpoint.

There are several other basic debug routines
which PEBUG provides for control and debug processing:

IFEQ, IFGE, IFGT, IFLE, IFLT, and IFNE
are conditional processors. A debug
routine can be invoked conditionally
using one of these processors. Two
parameters are compared to determine
whether the specified routine is to be
called.

JUP and LAB are processors used to provide
a primitive type of branch logic. These
processors have meaning only when the
commands originate from a file (FIL).

DEF is a processor to define local debugging symbols.

DIS and DMP are processors used for displaying blocks of central memory.

SET is the processor used to modify the
contents of central memory locations.

WRIT is the processor used to provide
debug time output.

STP is the stop processor. This routine
is used to terminate debugging.

As has been mentioned, any routine can be given
control by entering the appropriate command. The
manner in which parameters are passed needs to be
considered. The processor CALL provides standard
Fortran (RUN) calling sequence linkage. The PEBUG
command scanner uses a parameter block calling
sequence. That is, a processor invoked directly by
a PEBUG command is given pointers to parameter
blocks in which the parameters are found. There
are currently five pointers passed. The first
points to a block which contains the parameters as
specified in the PEBUG command. The other four are
pointers to blocks of system information maintained

by the breakpoint interpreter and which otherwise
would not normally be available.

The output generated at debug time is written
on a "BUGOUT" file rather than the standard OUTPUT
file. A record of all debugging commands is also
written on the BUGOUT file. This debugging record
is written independently of the source of the debug
command. This procedure not only gives a history
of the debugging performed for non-interactive jobs
but also provides a hard copy history for the interactive jobs.

The PEBUG system is initially given control
after program loading is complete and before
execution begins. This is done by simply setting
a load switch (BUG) which the loader examines. If
the switch is set, the loader saves the normal program transfer point and gives control to PEBUG. If
and when PEBUG is given a GO command, execution will
begin at the normal transfer point as saved by the
loader. When PEBUG gets initial control, it does
some initialization procedures and then simply
performs the following command:

FIL, 'BUGIN', 0

This command simply starts processing debugging
commands from record zero of a file called BUGIN.
From this point on, control and execution flow is
determined by the command scanner and the breakpoint/
interpreter.

THE COMMANDS

We shall discuss the calling sequences of the
PEBUG commands and also give a few examples of the
use of each. The name of each command appears first
in capitals followed by the list of parameters in
lower case letters.

AT,*breakpoint address,processor address,parameter,*
    ...,parameter

AT sets a breakpoint to give control to the specified debugging subroutine.

    e.g.   AT,MAIN/100,DIS,MAIN/A
          This command sets a breakpoint at
          labeled location 100 in program
          MAIN to display the variable A.

    e.g.   AT,SUB+1,TRM
          This command sets a breakpoint to
          give interactive control to a
          terminal whenever the subroutine
          SUB is entered.

CALL, *processor address,parameter,...,parameter*

CALL calls a Fortran subroutine with conventional
calling sequence.

    e.g.   CALL,DUMP,PROG/I,*+100D
          This command calls a subroutine
          with a standard Fortran calling
          sequence to dump 101 decimal words
          of an array I in the program PROG.

CKP, *primary level number* (defaults to zero),
    secondary level number (defaults to zero),
    pointer to file name (defaults to the file
    $CKPNT)

CKP takes a checkpoint dump.

    e.g.   CKP
          This command takes a checkpoint
          dump with level numbers of zero
          and writes it to the default
          file $CKPNT.

    e.g.   CKP,1
          This command takes a checkpoint
          dump on the file $CKPNT with a
          primary level number of one.

```
      e.g.  CKP,21,45,'CHECK'
            This command takes a checkpoint
            dump on the file CHECK with
            primary level number 21 and
            secondary level number 45.
```

CRT

CRT begins to take debugging commands from the CDC
252 cathode ray tube display terminal.

```
      e.g.  CRT
            This command gives interactive
            debugging control to the CDC 252.
```

DBG,*central address of command list*

DBG begins to take debugging commands from central
memory. The commands are stored consecutively with
a low order 12-bit byte of a word indicating the
end of a line and a zero word indicating the end of
the list.

```
      e.g.  DBG,BLOCK/COM
            This command begins executing
            debug commands from a data block
            called COM in the program block
            BLOCK.
```

DEF,*pointer to symbol name,address definition*
            (defaults to a system defined location)

DEF defines a local symbol to represent any specified address or if none is specified then also
reserves an internal termporary location.

```
      e.g.  DEF,"LL1"
            This command defines a local
            symbol LL1.

      e.g.  DEF,'SW',SQRT/A+(MAIN/INDEX)
            This command defines a local
```

symbol SW to represent the
address of word in an array A
in the program SQRT. The particular word is displayed in the
array by a quantity stored in a
location called INDEX within
the program MAIN.

DIS,*FWA of central memory block,LWA of central
    memory block* (defaults to *, i.e. the first
        parameter value)

DIS displays a central memory block.

    e.g.   DIS,2
           This command displays the
           location 2.

    e.g.   DIS,/CC1/,*+10B
           The command displays 11 octal
           locations of a common block
           called CC1.

DMP,*FWA of block,LWA of block* (if none dump block
    0-FWA)

DMP uses the system dump routine to dump a block of
central memory to the OUTPUT file.

    e.g.   DMP,40000.
           This command dumps the central
           memory block of 0 to 40000 to
           the OUTPUT file.

    e.g.   DMP,MAIN/,*+1000B
           This command dumps 1000 octal words
           of the program block MAIN.

FIL,*pointer to file name,record number*   (defaults
    to zero)

FIL begins to take debugging commands from a specified logical record on a specified file.

    e.g.   FIL,'BUGIN'
            This command begins executing
            debug commands from record zero
            of the file BUGIN.

    e.g.   FIL,'BUG18',6
            This command begins executing
            debug commands from record 6
            of the file BUG18.

GO,*program address*   (defaults to the address next
        in normal execution)

GO begins program execution.

    e.g.   GO
            This command begins execution from
            where it was last interrupted.

    e.g.   GO,MAIN/+1
            This command begins execution at
            the first location in the program
            block MAIN.

IFEQ, IFGE, IFGT, IFLE, IFLT and IFNE,*first value*
        to be compared, second value to be compared,
        processor address, parameter,...,parameter

IFEQ, IFGE, IFGT, IFLE, IFLT and IFNE conditionally
invokes the specified debugging routine.

    e.g.   IFEQ,(MAIN/J),O,DIS,MAIN/K
            This command conditionally
            displays the variable K in the
            program MAIN if the variable J
            is zero.

    e.g.   IFLT,(MAIN/I)+(MAIN/J),(MAIN/K),CRT
            This command conditionally gives
            debugging control to the CDC 252
            if the sum of the variables I

and J in the program MAIN is
less than the variable K in the
program MAIN.

INT, Program address (defaults to the address next
    in normal execution)

INT begins interpretive program execution. The
execution switch is set for interpretive execution
and a GO command issued.

JMP,*target label address*

JMP causes the scanner to skip commands until the
proper LAB command is encountered. This command
is   effect only if the commands are currently
being received from a file, i.e. via a FIL command.

        e.g.   JMP,1
               This command causes control to
               skip to the next LAB,1 command
               and then proceed.

LAB,*label address*

LAB is normally a no-operation instruction unless
a JMP instruction with the same label has been
executed.

        e.g.   LAB,13
               This command will do nothing
               unless a JMP,13 command was
               executed earlier in the sequence
               of commands.

RES,*primary level number*   (defaults to zero),
    secondary level number (defaults to zero),
    pointer to file name (defaults to the file
        $CKPNT)

RES restores central memory from a previous check-point.

> e.g.   RES
> This command restores central
> memory from a checkpoint dump
> with zero level identifiers on
> the file $CKPNT.

> e.g.   RES,21,45,'CHECK'
> This command restores central
> memory from a checkpoint dump
> with level identifiers of 21
> and 45 on the file CHECK.

RMV, pointer to trap type (the types include: B-breakpoint, L-load, S-simple, F-flow, C-call, V-variable, E-error), *first conditional specified, second conditional specified*   (see Figure 2)

RMV removes a breakpoint or interpretive trap.

> e.g.   RMV,'B',SUB/10
> This command removes a breakpoint
> at location 10 of the subroutine
> SUB.

> e.g.   RMV,'V',TEST/A,TEST/B
> This command removes a variable
> trace on the block of variables
> from A to B in the program TEST.

> e.g.   RMV,'L',1,2
> This command removes a load trap
> for overlay 1,2.

> e.g.   RMV,'E'
> This command remvoes error traps.

SET,*central memory address,contents to be stored*

SET sets the contents of the specified central
memory location.

> e.g.   SET,PROG/L,1
>   This command sets the variable
>   L in the program PROG to one.

STP

STP stops debugging. The debugging files are
properly closed and program execution ended.

> e.g.   STP
>   This command stops debugging.

TRAP,*pointer to trap type*   (the types include:
    L-load, S-simple, F-flow, C-call, V-variable,
    E-error), *first conditional, second condi-
    tional* (see Figure 2), *processor address,
    parameter,...,parameter*

TRAP sets an interpretive trap to give control to
the specified debugging subroutine.

> e.g.   TRAP,'S',SUB/,SUBR/,DIS,SUB/I
>   This command sets a simple trace
>   trap for the block of locations
>   from the first of the program
>   SUB to the first of the program
>   SUBR to display the variable I in
>   the subroutine SUB.

> e.g.   TRAP,'V',0,100B,TRM
>   This command sets a variable
>   trap for the first 100 octal
>   locations of central memory
>   to give interactive control to
>   a teletype.

TRM

TRM begins to take debugging commands from a teletype terminal.

     e.g.   TRM
            This command gives interactive
            debugging control to a teletype.

WRIT,*pointer to first word of the line*

WRIT writes a line to the BUGOUT file.

     e.g.   WRIT,' THIS IS A DEBUG OUTPUT LINE'
            This command writes the line "THIS
            IS A DEBUG OUTPUT LINE" on the
            BUGOUT file.

XEQ,*program address*   (defaults to the address next
       in normal execution)

XEQ begins regular program execution. The execution
switch is set for regular execution and a GO command
issued.

CONCLUSION

     At present the PEBUG system is performing quite
well. The system has been used on several experimental problems with satisfactory results. The
original design goals have been met, and we hope to
release the system for general use at Purdue University by the end of this year (1970).

*The research described in this paper was partially
supported by Control Data Corporation under a research grant to the Purdue University Computing
Center.

DEBUGGING UNDER SIMULATION

Robert M. Supnik
Applied Data Research

An argument is made for the extensive use of interactive simulation as a debugging tool in the development of programming systems for small machines. Applied Data Research's simulation system MIMIC is described and a discussion of the debugging commands is presented.

SIMULATION AS A DEBUGGING TOOL

Given the ubiquity of mini- and midicomputers today, I imagine that many of you here have designed or implemented complex systems for this class of machine. Thus, you are already familiar with the horrors which await the programmer faced with the task of building complex software for simple processors. For those who have not experienced this particular form of mental anguish, I would like to illustrate some of the problems facing the small machines' programmer.

Three years ago, I was working on a television-station control system designed around a PDP-8. The program occupied all but 200 words in core, so there was no room for ODT or DDT or some similar debugging package. Further, the system consisted of ten

independent jobs running under the control of a
multi-programming interrupt-driven monitor, so any
standard debugging package would simply have died.
At one point in the debugging, a curious circumstance
arose — given a specific set of conditions, the
system more or less cleared itself to zero, leaving
absolutely no clue as to what had started the massa-
cre or how it had been propagated. Worse yet, stra-
tegically placed HALT instructions failed to isolate
the problem, since, as it turned out, all the obvious
suspects were innocent.

Again: a year ago, some of my colleagues were
finishing a disk-based software system for the PDP-8.
This system exhibited the following peculiar symptom:
on some occasions it ran perfectly, without a failure; on others, it crashed as soon as it was started.
Why? It happened that the disk scheduling algorithm
was sensitive to the initial disk latency that is,
to the position of the disk at the moment the program
was started. It was impossible to force the failure
to occur, since the position of the real disk at
startup could not be controlled.

Finally: for the past year, I have been working on a small-scale time-sharing system for controlling several analytical instruments. The basic problem with this sytem is that by the time any bug
manifests itself in the form of a report of a system
crash, the system component which caused the bug has
been swapped out of core and overwritten by another
component, thereby obliterating all the evidence as
to what went wrong.

And so it goes — a clobbered word which is
allegedly never accessed, a process suddenly coming
to a dead halt without leaving any trace of what
stopped it or why, data structures mysteriously
pointing to each other instead of to the data, and
so on. Against such bugs, the programmer has little
recourse except to curse the so-called debugging
software and to develop dexterity at manipulating
the computer's console switches.

Simulation offers a way out of the typical

small machine limitations of no core, no help, and
virtually no hope. After I explain why, I will
briefly describe ADR's PDP-10 based simulation system, MIMIC, and show how it answers the questions
raised by the theory.

The systems group at ADR began using simulators
for debugging with only vague ideas of the benefits
which would be gained; the theoretical justification
for the idea was not considered until recently.
Therefore, this "theory" is neither complete nor
objective, but rather inductive — an abstraction,
as it were, from collective experience.

The problems of debugging can roughly be reduced to three: *access, control*, and *repeatability/
impossibility*. I will take each of these up in
turn.

The problem of *access* is the problem of getting
at and possibly modifying the data items which are
the contents of hardware units such as: core memory
locations, central processor (CPU) registers, disk
words, and so on. Most minicomputer debugging tools
make only a very limited attempt at solving this
problem. A typical small machine debugging package
will allow the user to examine and change core and
perhaps also one or two programmable registers. The
user is usually on his own in matters dealing with
the disk, the paper-tape punch, or inadequate core
for a debugging package.

Clearly, that is inadequate. Far too often,
the user finds that what he really needs to examine
is the disk or the paper-tape punch. In the former
case, with the disk, he is out of luck completely,
unless he builds his own special purpose debugging
routine, which would take up valuable core; with the
paper-tape punch, he has no resources but to tedi-
ously count characters until he finds the one he
wants — a painful experience indeed if the tape
contains ten or twenty thousand characters!

Of course, a small machine debugging package
really cannot provide access to all possible devices.

First of all, some devices are inaccessible; the
paper-tape punch cannot be read and rewritten.
Secondly, a small machine system cannot afford the
core needed for device-dependent access, especially
since each device probably requires unique and
peculiar handling.

A simulator, on the other hand, can overcome
both of these problems. First, I/O device input
and output can be kept on the host computer's disk;
that is, the simulated devices can read from and
write onto disk files. Thus, the input to, and output from, simulated devices never become physically
or logically inaccessible to the simulator system.
Second, the simulator's debugging package resides
not in simulated core but in the host machine's
core; therefore, the debugging package can grow as
large and as complicated as necessary without im-
pinging on the program being debugged.

A simulator has a similar advantage over the
real machine with respect to registers. The real
machine can only make available those registers which
it itself can access, that is, the *programmable*
registers. The simulator, on the other hand, can
make everything available — programmable registers,
internal registers, invented registers. A simulator
can thus not only provide complete information about
the current state of the system being simulated, but
also through judicious invention of new registers,
information about past states as well.

In sum, not only can a simulator provide more
complete access facilities, but also more sophisticated facilities. In a properly designed simulator,
any data item of any simulated device can be examined, modified, searched, dumped, or breakpointed
just like core memory. Such a data item will be
designated a *frame*.

It may seem unnecessary to be able to search
and dump I/O devices just like core memory. In
many debugging situations, admittedly, such facilities would not be needed; but in those where they
are useful, they are usually vital. For example, in

debugging a disk-based system, if a disk-output
operation goes awry and output disappears into
hyperspace, it would be difficult and extraordinarily
time-consuming to find out with ordinary debugging
tools exactly where the output was written on the
disk. However, if the disk can be searched and partially or completely dumped, the task of locating
the errant record would obviously be much simpler.

A simulator's enormous advantages with respect
to access are repeated with respect to control.
Control, by far the worst debugging headache, is the
problem of handling a dynamic process, of directing,
altering or interrupting a program while it is running. Small machine debugging packages offer only
the most limited help with control problems — at
best, a small number of breakpoints which work only
if the breakpointed location is fetched as an instruction. If the program overwrites a flagged
location, the breakpoint is lost and the user is
too. Further, virtually no small machine debugging
package can survive in a real-time environment.
Most of them will not tolerate interrupts and also
tend to disrupt I/O device operations irrevocably.
In a real-time system, such disruptions invariably
mean that operations cannot be resumed after a debugging break but must instead be restarted.

Simulators need not suffer these problems.
First, in a properly designed simulator, debugging
interruptions are totally transparent to the program
being simulated. The user can interrupt execution
whenever or however he chooses, poke around inside
the simulator, and then, barring deliberate changes,
resume simulation at exactly the same point and
with the simulated machine in exactly the same state
as when the interruption occurred. Nothing need be
changed or lost.

Second, a simulator can provide enormously more
complex control mechanisms than the real machine.
The superiority of simulation derives from two
factors: one, the simulated memory can have an extra
bit, or several extra bits, devoted exclusively to
debugging purposes; and two, the simulator can detect

and flag questionable machine states which the real
machine normally cannot or does not detect.   The
extra bit is the necessary keystone of a good breakpoint mechanism and trap machanism.

    In its most general form, a *breakpoint* is a
flag associated with a frame.   More specifically, a
breakpoint is usually a flag which tells the CPU or
I/O device to interrupt execution and *break* to the
debugging package whenever the flagged frame is
accessed in a certain way.   With a simulator, breakpoints need not be limited to the instruction execution phase but can be set for any accessing con-
text.   The following list illustrates the kinds of
breakpoints which can be implemented in a simulator.
The break names are as used in MIMIC, which is described in the second part of this paper.

> E-break: if accessed as instruction
> N-break: if accessed as indirection vector
> R-break: if read by the CPU
> W-break: if written into by the CPU
> I-break: if used as input operand by a
>   direct-memory-access (DMA) device
> O-break: if used as output operand by a
>   DMA device

The complexity of the breakpoint mechanism is limited
only by the ingenuity of the simulator's designers,
since the breakpoint mechanism takes no room in simulated core.   Useful breakpoint features might
include proceed counts on breaks and the ability to
associate user-defined commands (called *actions* —
analagous to indirect statements in JOSS) with
breaks.   The action facility would enable the user
to specify one or more commands which would be executed when a break occurs; the user could thus set
up traces, overlays, dumps, etc., in connection with
breakpoints.

    Whereas breakpoints are flags on differing con-
ditions in specific frames, traps are breaks on
specific conditions regardless of which frame is
being accessed.   The conditions which are trapped by
a simulator would obviously depend on the machine

being simulated, but the following might constitute
a minimum set:

> external interruption trap: trap to the
> debugging package at the beginning
> of the next instruction cycle in
> response to a user request (such as
> striking a special teletype key)

> single instruction trap: trap at the
> beginning of every instruction cycle
> (controlled by a user-accessible
> debugging flag)

> halt trap: trap if instruction being
> executed involves a central proces-
> sor halt

> illegal instruction trap: trap if the
> instruction being executed is un-
> defined or illegal

> illegal memory reference trap: trap if
> the instruction being executed refer-
> ences non-existent core.

Further, the springing of these traps can be made
conditional on user-accessible debugging flags, so
that if the user does not want a condition trapped,
he can disable the trap-out to the simulator's debugging package.

As with access and control, a simulator is
essential in attempting to deal with the related debugging problems of *repeatability* and *impossibility*.
Repeatability is shorthand for the problem of repro-
ducing on demand a particular machine state (particularly the one that blew your program). Such
reproduction of a particular state is simply impossible on the real machine, if only because CPU
and I/O device timing are subject to variation,
sometimes as much as +20%. These timing fluctuations
do not occur under simulation (unless the user delib-
erately sets them up). An instruction always executes in the same amount of *simulated* time; an I/O

operation always runs for the same amount of time.
Further, under simulation, a particular machine
state can be saved and restored as desired, whereas
on the real machine, at best only core storage and
the programmable registers can be saved and restored.

The other side of repeatability is impossibility — the problem of introducing unexpected, perhaps even impossible, variations into a given machine state. Clearly, it is utterly impossible for
the real machine or any real-machine debugging
package to produce a given machine state on cue,
especially if that machine state violates the state-
constraints implicit in the hardware. On the other
hand, it is possible and usually easy to produce a
predefined machine state under simulation. All the
variables involved in defining a machine state —
device flags, internal registers, etc. — are user-
accessible. To set up a machine state, the user
needs merely to interrupt his program by breakpoint
or trap, manipulate the important registers or
frames, and then restart or continue simulation.
He can also save the state of the simulated machine
for further recall and refinement.

Under simulation all key variables are user-
accessible. For example, in a properly designed
simulator, the user would be able to position a
serial device, such as the paper-tape reader or
punch, over a specific character in the input or
output stream before starting simulation. More
importantly, the user would be able to alter the
timing characteristics of individual devices as
desired. While the real machine's teleprinter
always times out in 110 milliseconds, the user could
set up the simulated teleprinter to time out after
an interval ranging from zero simulated seconds on
up past several simulated minutes. He would be able
to specify that the simulated disk spin six times
or ten times or half as fast as the real disk, or
that the simulated paper-tape reader read 100,000
characters per second, or that the line frequency
clock tick at 50 Hz instead of 60; he can, literally,
do anything he chooses.

To recapitulate, the basic case for simulation
is that a simulator can fully handle the most important debugging problems — access, control, repeat-
ability/impossibility — while a real-machine debugging system can only touch on the edges of these
problems. Of course, a programmer may not need
such complex debugging tools as a simulator can
offer. If he is writing BASIC programs on a small
machine time-sharing system, simulation is totally
pointless. However, if he were working on the BASIC
compiler, a simulator would be most useful, and if
he were debugging the time-sharing system itself, a
simulator might be damned near essential.

It can be argued of course that instead of using
a simulator the user could outfit the real machine
with extra core, a line printer, and the other additions necessary to expand a small machine into one
sufficiently powerful for use in program development.
However, for implementers of dedicated systems and
any other type of program in which debugging is a
major cost, such a course of action does not make
economic sense. First of all, in a dedicated system,
the extra hardware added solely for program development, such as the line printer, will be useless once
the program is checked out and the machine is in
full-time use as a dedicated processor. Secondly,
in general, all the extra hardware will not cut down
debugging time but will merely make bare-bones
assembly and debugging possible.

Finally, the programmer will still have to deal
with the inherent limitations of debugging on the
real hardware and with the man-made limitations of
making do with the usual worthless small machine
software. These problems can be overcome by editing,
assembling, and debugging small machine systems on
larger, host computers. A host computer programming
system can offer the small machine programmer not
only a more viable debugging environment in the form
of a simulator, but also a better program development
environment in the form of sophisticated editors and
assemblers.

MIMIC

MIMIC is ADR's simulation system for small and medium-scale computers. It runs interactively on the PDP-10 under the standard time-sharing monitors and currently handles the following computers: Digital Equipment Corporation PDP-8/I, PDP-8/E, PDP-7/9/15; Data General Corporation Nova, Supernova, Nova 800, Nova 1200, and Supernova SC; Foxboro FOX-1.

The first point to be mentioned is that *MIMIC itself is not a simulator;* it is a support package and operating environment for simulators. A typical debugging simulator consists of three parts: a hardware simulator, a simulated-machine to host-machine I/O interface, and a debugging package. The last two comprise MIMIC proper and are the same for all simulators in our system; the first must be hand-coded for each simulator.

The standardization of the debugging package and the I/O interface is possible because MIMIC proper views and handles all simulated or virtual machines in terms of an abstract model. From MIMIC's point of view, a *virtual machine* is merely a collection of autonomous code modules called *controllers*. Each controller corresponds more or less to an actual hunk of hardware — a typical simulator for a small machine might have controllers for the central processor (CPU), keyboard (TTI), teleprinter (TTO), paper-tape reader (PTR), paper-tape punch (PTP), disk or drum (DSK or DRM), etc. In turn, each controller is made up of *registers* and *units*. A register is a named variable; a unit a source of input *frames* (such as transport in a multi-drive magnetic tape system). Frames are numbered, rather than named variables, and are expected to be organized in a file and ordered by frame-numbers. A unit need not have a frame set (simulated clocks do not); a controller need not have any registers.

In many cases, such as for the central processor or the paper-tape reader, the controller and unit are logically the same and are only formally distinct for purposes of standardization; however, this need not be true.

     MIMIC treats all controllers and units identically; hence, any controller-oriented command can be applied to any controller or unit in the system.

     To show the debugging commands available under MIMIC, we will use the implementation for the Digital PDP-8/I. This set of examples is illustrative of the tools MIMIC provides but by no means exhausts the resources available to the user. In the examples, the following typographic conventions will be used:

     *   typed out by MIMIC to request user input

              italicized type is output typed by MIMIC

     [cr]   represents the CARRIAGE RETURN key

     [lf]   represents the LINE FEED key

     ↑char represents the control character produced by holding down the CTRL button and striking the indicated character.

1. Loading Programs: binary files produced by the various PDP-10 based small machine assemblers can be loaded directly into simulated core by the LOAD command:

     *LOAD DSKSYS.BIN[cr]   or
     *LOAD TAPE1,TAPE2,HISFIL 101,102[cr]

2. Starting simulation:

     *START 200[cr]   power clear the simulated
                      machine and start simulation
                      at 200

     *RUN 3041[cr]   start simulation at 3041
                      without power clear

3. Interrupting simulation: simulation may be interrupted in any of the following ways:

a) VM detects a breakpoint (see below);
b) CPU decodes a HALF instruction;
c) User types ↑E (wru) on the console
   teletype (simulation is interrupted at
   the start of the next fetch cycle);
d) CPU decodes an illegal instruction;
e) CPU or I/O device references non-
   existent memory.

Each interruption results in a unique type-out and
a restart of the debugging package.

4. Continuing simulation: simulation may be resumed
after an interruption by using GO or CONTINUE:

        *GO[cr]   or   *CON[cr]

5. Associating data files with simulated devices:
the ATTACH command is used to associate a file with
a simulated device or to find out about the current
association:

        *ATT PTR←INPUT.BIN[cr]   associate INPUT.BIN
                                      with the simulated
                                      PTR

        *ATT DSK? *SRFDSK*   find out which file
                                      is associated with
                                      the simulated disk

        *ATT PTP/ *OUTPUT* *OUTPUT.1[cr]
                                      examine and modify
                                      the file associated
                                      with the simulated
                                      PTP

        *ATT SYS?   examine the status of
        CPU/   *NOT ATTACHABLE* all simulated devices.
        PTR/   *UNATTACHED*   The keyboard (TKB)
        PTP/   *UNATTACHED*   and teleprinter (TTY)
        TKB/   *CTY*   are attached to the
        TTY/   *CTY*   user's console tele-
        DSK/   *MYDSK*   type.

6. Closing data files associated with simulated

devices: the DETACH command is used to break the
association between a simulated device and a data
file:

    *DETACH PTR,PTP[cr] detach the files
                             associated with the
                             simulated PTP and PTR

    *DETACH ALL[cr]   detach all attached
                             files

7.   Examining and modifying frames and registers:
within any controller, any set of frames and/or
registers can be collectively or individually examined or modified.

    *ALL←0[cr]   clear all frames of the
                             default unit (usually
                             the CPU: see next section)

    *DSK STATE?   print all registers in
                             the simulated disk

    *PTR 1-4,5,7,100-102,RF?
                             print paper-tape reader
                             frames 1 through 4,5,7,
                             100 through 102, and also
                             the register RF

    *AC/ *0101* *0[cr]   print and allow the user
                             to modify register AC

    *CPU 2-3:   allow the user to modify
                             the indicated frames
    2:   *4444[cr]
    3:   *0[cr]

    300/ *1234* *1233[lf] When typing frame input,
    301/ *2377* */*   the user can type a
    2377/ *1010* *↑*   special terminator to
    2376/ *0246* *@*   alter control flow:
    2246/ *0000* *[cr]   [lf]=go to next frame;
                              ↑ =go to previous
                               frame;
                           / =go to frame pointed

                                        at by current
                                        frame;
                              @ =go to frame addressed
                                    by current
                                    frame.

8. Modifying the default unit: if no controller
or unit is specified in an examination/modification
command, the default unit is sued. Initially, the
default unit is the CPU, but this can be changed
with the UNIT command.

> *UNIT/ *CPU* *PTR[cr] examine and change the
>   default unit
>
> *UNIT? *PTR*   print out the default
>   unit
>
> *UNIT←CPU[cr]   or   change the default unit
>
> *UNIT: *CPU[cr]

9. Searching frames and registers: frames and
registers can be searched for the presence or absence of certain conditions, and the normal examin-
ation/modification variants (/ : ? and ←) applied
only to those frames or registers which pass the
specified test:

> *SEARCH ALL FOR 6134←7000[cr]
>   search the default unit
>   (the CPU) for all frames
>   whose value is 6134 and
>   change them to 7000
>
> *SEARCH PTR 0-400 for NE 200?
>   list those paper-tape
>   reader frames in the
>   range 0-400 whose value
>   is not 200
>
> *SEARCH CPU 100,200-256 FOR AND 77 = 40/
>   print out and allow the
>   user to modify all CPU
>   frames in the indicated

                           range whose low order
                           six bits equal 40

*SEARCH DSK STATE FOR NE 0?
                           print all non-zero disk
                           registers

10. Dumping frames and registers: frames and
registers of any controller may be dumped to a disk
file for later printing using the DUMP command.

*DUMP CORDMP.LST CPU STATE,ALL[cr]
                           dump all of core and
                           all central processor
                           registers to file
                           CORDMP.LST

*DUMP SECTOR DSK 200-377[cr]
                           dump the indicated frames
                           to file SECTOR

11. Setting and clearing breakpoints: MIMIC offers
six types of breakpoints, namely, E, N, R, W, I, and
0, as described in the first part. These breakpoints
may be set and cleared using the BREAK command.

*BREAK←200-210←E[cr]   set E-breakpoints at
                           locations 200-210

*BREAK 200/←E *N[cr]   print out the breakpoint
                           at 200 and   an N-
                           breakpoint

*BREAK 207-214←[cr]   remove all breakpoints
                           in locations 207-214

*BREAK 5432:   *-R,W[cr]
                           remove the R-breakpoint
                           at 5432 and add a W-
                           breakpoint

*BREAK ALL?   print all breakpoints
                           set in core (locations
                           without any breakpoints
                           are not printed)

The user can also specify a breakpoint proceed-count.
If the proceed count is 'n', the breakpoint is not
reported to the user until the 'n'th time it is
detected. A proceed-count of zero or one means by
convention "break every time." Proceed-counts are
set with the BREAK command:

    *BREAK 200/   E,N   *(20)[cr]
                                 add a proceed-count of
                                 20 to the breakpoint at
                                 location 200

    *BREAK 404←(0)[cr]   zero the proceed-count
                                 of the breakpoint at
                                 location 404

The user can also associate actions with breakpoints.
Actions are user-specified, numbered commands which,
if associated with a breakpoint, are executed whenever that breakpoint is detected (for specification
of actions, see the next section). Actions are
matched with breakpoints using the BREAK command:

    *BREAK 200/   E,N(20) *;1,2,c[cr]
                                 add actions 1,2,and 'c'
                                 (predefined as CONTINUE)
                                 to the breakpoint at 200

    *BREAK 1000-1777←W,0;-1,-2,4,27[cr]
                                 add W- and 0- breakpoints
                                 and actions 4 and 27 to
                                 the specified breakpoints
                                 and remove actions 1 and
                                 2 from the specified
                                 breakpoints

    *BREAK 12203:   *;-[cr]
                                 remove all actions from
                                 the breakpoint at 12203
                                 without disturbing the
                                 break conditions

    *BREAK 507:   *-;[cr]

                                 remove all break condi-
                                 tions from the breakpoint

                              at 507 without disturb-
                              ing the actions

12. Specifying actions: with the exception of 'c',
which is predefined as CONTINUE, the user must
specify the commands to be used as actions. The
ACTION command is used to define and examine actions:

      *ACTION 1: *AC,MQ?   define action 1

      *ACTION 2,SEARCH ALL FOR 6032?
                              define action 2

      *ACTION 22/*LOAD NXTPHS*
                              examine and modify
                              action 22

      ACTION 22/ LOAD NXTPHS.BIN[cr]

      *ACTION 1,2,22-35?   print the indicated
                              actions

      *ACTION ALL?   print all defined
                              actions

      *ACTION ALL←[cr]   clear (set to undefined)
                              all actions

The user may specify up to thirty-five actions.

13. Executing actions: actions may be executed
from command level using the DO command:

      *DO 2,5-11,31[cr]   execute the indicated
                              actions

DO commands can be nested, that is, DO commands can
be executed from action buffers:

      *ACTION 1←100-137?   define action 1 to dump
                              result array

      *ACTION 2←LOAD NXTPHS.BIN[cr]
                              define action 2 to get
                              next phase

```
    *ACTION 3←ATTACH DSK NEWDSK[cr]
                              define action 3 to attach
                              next phase disk file

    8action 4←DO 1-3[cr]      define action 4 to do
                              all next phase actions

    *DO 4[cr]                 get next phase
```

14. Saving and restoring a machine state: the
current machine state, including all registers, core
memory, all breakpoints, all defined actions, and
the state of all busy or attached devices, can be
saved using the SAVE command:

```
    *SAVE GOODRN[cr]          save the current machine
                              state in file GOODRN.MIM
                              (extension automatically
                              provided)
```

Conversely, a saved machine state can be restored
using the GET command:

```
    *GET GOODRN[cr]           restore the machine state
                              specified in file
                              GOODRN.MIM
```

15. Resetting devices: simulated controllers can
be reset to their "clear" or "power up" state using
the RESET command:

```
    *RESET TKB,DSK[cr]        reset the simulated
                              keyboard and disk

    *RESET ALL[cr]            reset the entire simu-
                              lated machine
```

16. Renaming controllers and units: controllers
and units can be renamed using the RENAME command:

```
    *RENAME C=CPU[cr]         change the name of the
                              CPU controller to C

    *RENAME D=DSK DSK[cr]     change the name of the
                              DSK unit to D
```

17. Comments: any line beginning with ; is treated
as a comment and ignored by MIMIC. Comments can be
placed in action buffers.

     *ACTION 34←;ATTEMPT TO WRITE READ-ONLY CORE![cr]

     *BREAK 14000-17777←W,0;34[cr]
                         define locations 14000-
                         17777 as read-only memory

     *START 200[cr]

     W-BREAK AT CPU 15717 attempt to write in
                         read-only core

     ;ATTEMPT TO WRITE READ-ONLY CORE!
                         core is flagged when
     *   action is "executed"

18. Leaving simulation: when finished with simulation, the user can assure an orderly exit from
MIMIC by using the QUIT command:

     *QUIT[cr]   leave MIMIC

     .   back at the PDP-10 Monitor

19. Miscellaneous debugging features:

     OLDPC   a register which records the value
                 of the program counter before the
                 last jump or subroutine-call instruc-
                 tion was executed.

     SINGLE   a flag which, if set to 1, places
                 the simulator in single-instruction
                 mode.

     TM   a register which records the elapsed
                 simulated time in CPU clock ticks
                 since the last START or RESET ALL
                 command.

The above examples merely provide an overview of the
common features available in all simulators imple-

mented under MIMIC. The actual devices and registers available to the user depend, of course, on
the machine being simulated and the machine config-
uration chosen.

DISCIPLINED SOFTWARE TESTING

W. R. Elmendorf
IBM Systems Development Division

I will talk this morning about some lessons we've learned from testing large, complex software systems. Actually, I believe these lessons are equally applicable to small software packages. While the large systems are admittedly particularly vulnerable to error, the small systems may have many more users and thus the impact of error can be equally great.

Before I go any further, let me distinguish be between testing and debugging. Many different definitions of these terms are in use. To me, *testing* determines that an error exists; *debugging* localizes the cause of error. I will be talking about the former.

I will be addressing functional testing but not performance testing. Just as performance testing involves space and time measures of system *utilization*, so functional testing involves spatial and temporal measures of system *quality*:

(a) The temporal measure is expressed as the mean time between error occurrences.

   (b)   The spatial measure is expressed
            as the number of errors waiting to
            occur.

The latter — *spatial measurement of functional quality* — is my subject.

I will not discuss either the design or implementation phases of software development (where the quality is built in). Instead, I will focus attention on the testing phase (where the quality is measured). Even though I'm addressing only one side of the coin, I want you to recognize that they sink or swim together:

   (a)   If either the design or implementation is sloppy, then the testing bogs down in a morass of problems, difficult to identify, expensive to fix, and impossible to schedule.

   (b)   If the testing is sloppy, then there is little motivation to practice quality in the design and implementation phases. Managers favor the criteria of excellence against which they're being measured. Testing is quality measurement and thus, indirectly, quality motivation.

Software quality is the focus of attention from inside and outside the industry. In response to this attention, software testing is evolving from the "testing is an art" philosophy toward the "testing is a discipline" philosophy. To me, this evolution is both inevitable and essential:

   (a)   It's inevitable because innovative people are never content to leave to chance that which can be controlled. They are always striving to harness and direct their energies. This implies increasing discipline.

(b)   It's essential, because without
      discipline in all phases of de-
      velopment, we simply won't be
      able to produce future software
      systems at a quality level accept-
      able to future users. My exper-
      ience with OS/360 convinces me of
      this premise; your presence at
      this symposium evidences your
      concurrence with it.

The body of this talk is well covered by my
paper published in the IEEE Transactions on Systems
Science and Cybernetics, Vol. SSC-5, No. 4, October
1969, pp. 284-290. Here is the abstract from that
paper:

Abstract: Functional testing of operating
systems is in transition from a predominantly im-
precise art to an increasingly precise science.
The process that controls this testing is maturing
correspondingly. The laissez-faire approach is
giving way to a disciplined approach charactized by
rigorous definition of the test plan, systematic
control of the test effort, and objective quantita-
tive measurement of the test coverage. This paper
describes just such a disciplined test control
process, which is composed of five steps: 1) the
survey, which establishes the intended extent of
testing; 2) the identification, which creates a list
of functional variations eligible for testing;
3) the appraisal, which ranks and subsets the eligible variations so that test resources can be
directed at those with the higher payoff; 4) the
review, which calculates the test coverage of the
test case library; and 5) the monitor, which
verifies attainment of the planned test coverage.
Throughout the test process, specification testing
is distinguished from program testing.

APPLICATION OF DISCIPLINED SOFTWARE TESTING

Paul Schlender
IBM Systems Development Division

Many factors affect the ability to meet the objective established in the disciplined approach to testing. The design of the system is one of these factors. The techniques utilized during the various stages of testing is another. The impact of these factors on the verification of a system's functional integrity will be related to disciplined software testing discussed earlier.

Ed. Note: What follows is a condensation of the talk.

The "T.H.E." system implemented by Professor Dijkstra is an example of the proper approach to designing a "testable" system.[1] The method of system subdivision used in "T.H.E." system allows one to logically deduce that most of the theoretically possible system states are in fact irrelevant to system behavior. The relevant states turn out to be few, and only these states need to be explicitly tested in the implemented system.

Specifications are also an important factor

in disciplined software testing. Analysis of program errors indicates that over one-third of them are caused by incomplete or ambiguous specifications. This is caused by these specifications being written in the English language. Work such as Dr. Schwartz's is progressing toward defining a descriptive notation that is rigorous and complete. Until such a notation is available, this approach to software testing will not be completely successful.

The testing phases can be broken down into three types; unit, interface, and regression. Unit testing validates that the basic algorithms and routines are complete and correct. The tests are derived from analysis of internal specifications and the code. They are executed in a simulated system environment to isolate errors to specific functions being tested. Interface testing validates that the basic algorithms and routines are tied together correctly. The tests are derived from analysis of external specifications. They are executed in a simulated environment or their normal system environment, depending on the availability of total system function. Regression testing validates that a previous level of functional capability has been maintained. The tests are derived from analysis of external and internal specifications and the code. They are executed in the normal system environment.

All levels of testing are monitored to insure they reach their stated objectives. This then is the measure of the disciplined approach to software testing.

---

1.   Dijkstra, E.W., "The Structure of the "THE" multiprogramming system, *Comm. ACM* 11(1968) 341-346.

TESTING CONVERSATIONAL SYSTEMS

N. J. King
IBM Systems Development Division

*A brief description is presented of the HOOK
facility, the principal debugging tool available to
TSS/360 system programmers who are working on those
system modules which provide supervisor and system
services to a user. It is preceded by a summary of
the talk presented at the Symposium.*

The presentation focused on testing technique
and tools used in developing the components, integration testing, and field support of a large programming system. Mechanisms to maintain and techniques used to measure and evaluate the reliability
of the programming system were described. The
support facilities used in the debugging of TSS/360
were discussed. Various debugging mechanisms,
including virtual machines, were examined for their
limitations and advantages.

THE HOOK FACILITY

The HOOK facility is a debugging tool which has
been implemented under TSS/360 in order to aid

systems programmers in debugging system code without
requiring dedicated machine time. In TSS/360 much
of the systems programming which is necessary to
provide service to a user exists in a portion of his
virtual memory, but is available to him on a read-
only basis. This is necessary because the code is
shared among many users, and must be protected from
alteration to provide isolation among the users.
The HOOK facility allows certain of the modules
which exist in this shared memory to be "replaced"
in the sense that one user can execute his own
version of certain modules, while other users are
unaffected by his testing. The great value of this
facility stems from the fact that he may carry on
his testing while other users are on the system
without the danger of disturbing any of the other
users.

       This feature is accomplished by inserting a
"hook" into each of the modules which is part of the
shared virtual memory. Since the individual users
cannot alter the shared copy of the module, HOOK
provides a facility for transferring control to the
user's own copy of each of the modules being tested
whenever the system copy is entered. This requires
that the HOOK macro is present at every entry point
which is to be made available for dynamic testing/
replacement. This dynamic replacement of shared
copies of modules by private ones cannot take place
unless the HOOK is present in the shared copy.

       Assembling the HOOK into the code has no effect
until the specific entry point is "armed," or
actually replaced with a user's own version. This
arming involves three steps:

       1.   Removing the definition of the shared
       copy of the entry point from the dictionary
       used by the loader. This is necessary so
       that the next step can be executed using
       the standard system loading facility, and
       there is no conflict of duplicate names.

       2.   The user's copy of the module is loaded
       into the non-shared portion of his virtual

memory.

3. A flag is set which indicates that the
entry point has been armed, or replaced
with a private copy to be executed in place
of the shared copy.

The action of arming an entry point alters the
user's task in certain external aspects. Subsequently loaded references to the "hooked" entry point
are resolved to the new version of the module.
This includes references which may come from any
debugging controls which the programmer is using,
so that any patches which he makes are made in the
new copy.

The fact that an entry point has been HOOKed
is transparent to any modules which reference it.
Upon linking to an armed HOOK macro, control is
immediately passed to a module which determines
whether this particular entry point has been hooked.
If it has not, then control is immediately returned
to the shared copy of the module. If it has,
control is passed to the user's own copy.

The HOOK facility is particularly useful
because it is reusable. Within a single session a
programmer may HOOK a module, test it, unHOOK it,
reassemble it to correct errors, and then reHOOK it,
all without affecting any other users of the system.
Before HOOK was available, this involved using
dedicated machine time, and therefore considerably
more expense to get the same effect.

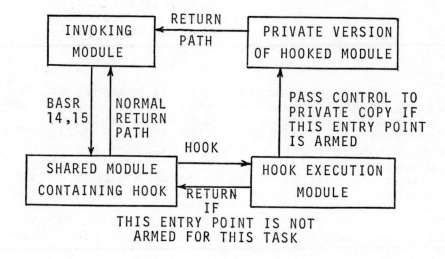

COMPILER CONSTRUCTION FOR DEBUGGING

R. Stockton Gaines
Institute for Defense Analysis
Princeton University

Ed. Note: What follows is a condensation of the talk. The content of Dr. Gaines' talk can be found in his Doctoral dissertation, "The Debugging of Computer Programs," *CRD Working Paper No. 266*, Institute for Defense Analyses, August 1969, from which the following abstract was taken. A book on debugging authored by Dr. Gaines is soon to appear from Prentice-Hall.

This thesis is a general study of the tools and techniques for debugging computer programs, and the design of compilers and operating systems to facilitate debugging. It includes an analysis of the programming process to identify carefully what the problems are in debugging and how they arise. Based on this analysis, the fundamental notions which underlie most debugging aids are identified. The facilities that are currently available to programmers using batch operating systems are discussed, and a number of new ones are presented.

The problems of debugging programs written in higher-level languages are considered in detail, and

the construction of compilers and programming languages for debugging receives careful attention. In
this connection, the topics of automatic error detection, language facilities which permit the programmer
to invoke debugging aids, and the compilation of code
in a manner appropriate for debugging in the program
are all discussed. A method is proposed to permit
the higher-level language programmer to debug his
program as if the language he wrote his program in
were the "machine language" of the computer which
executes the program, as a consequence of which the
programmer can receive the same kind of assistance
that is available to the machine language programmer.

The construction of interactive debugging
systems and operating system features necessary to
support advanced debugging facilities is discussed.
Three interactive debugging systems are considered
in detail, including one which was designed to work
with CRT consoles. A number of new ideas in this
are presented, and the considerable advantages of
interactive debugging are clearly demonstrated.